Management for Profess

Gregory Usher

Project Management in the 21ˢᵗ Century

What You Need to Know About
the Elephant, Eco-System
and Experience

 Springer

Gregory Usher
Enso Consulting
Lawnton, QLD, Australia

ISSN 2192-8096   ISSN 2192-810X   (electronic)
Management for Professionals
ISBN 978-3-030-71545-8   ISBN 978-3-030-71543-4   (eBook)
https://doi.org/10.1007/978-3-030-71543-4

This Springer imprint is published by the registered company Springer Nature Switzerland AG
The registered company address is: Gewerbestrasse 11, 6330 Cham, Switzerland

Contents

List of Figures

List of Tables

The Elephant

Oh, You're a Project Manager That's Nice. What Do You Do?

The purpose of this book is to challenge the way you think about project management. It will not make you better at scheduling or cost planning – but it might make you ask whether we should do these things. This book turns a spotlight on gaping holes in the current project management theory, and challenges you to think about project management in a whole new way. If you don't know why the Project Management Elephant, Eco-system and Experience are important, then this is the book for you.

It's not that I'm embarrassed by what I do, it's just that, well… I can never really explain it properly and that ends up making me look like an idiot. Here's how the conversation usually unfolds:

> *Party goer:* "So, Greg, what do you do?"
> *Me:* "I'm a project manager."
> *Party goer:* "Oh, a lot of people seem to be project managers these days. What exactly does a project manager do?"
> *Me:* "Well, specifically, I manage construction projects."
> *Party goer:* "Oh, so you're a builder?"
> *Me:* "Well, no. I don't actually build things – but I do spend a lot of my time resolving building issues."
> *Party goer:* "Oh, so more like an Architect?"
> *Me:* "Ummm, no I'm not a designer – but I do spend a lot of my time working with the designers."
> *Party goer:* "OK, so if you are not a builder or a designer, what does a project manager actually do?"

It's usually at this point that the whole conversation becomes a little strained. I mean how do I give an 'elevator pitch' to explain to the uninitiated exactly what my

© The Author(s), under exclusive license to Springer Nature Switzerland AG 2021
G. Usher, *Project Management in the 21ˢᵗ Century*, Management
for Professionals, https://doi.org/10.1007/978-3-030-71543-4_1

job as a project manager entails without saying something inane like 'project managers, manage projects'?

I usually resort to discussing the 'Iron Triangle', which of course I already assumes the person has some understanding of project management theory. Or I might make some sort of quip about how my job is like 'herding cats' or doing the things that no one else wants to do. Regardless of what I end up saying, I always feel like my explanation fails to capture the complexity of my role.

This problem of not being able to succinctly describe what I do led me on a journey of discovery regarding the profession of project management. On this journey, I found out that I'm not the only one who has trouble explaining what project managers 'do'. I found that there are many practitioners, researchers and academics out there who think that there is something fundamentally wrong with the way we perceive and understand our role. I learned about this problem called the 'praxis-theory gap' which is just a fancy way of saying that project managers spend a lot of their time doing things that no one ever told them was part of their job. I learned that, rather than developing our profession based on what we really do, we started our profession by choosing a ready-made theoretical foundation that looked like what we do and then proceeded to spend the next seven decades explaining why it's not really what we do. What's more, I discovered that this identity crisis has caused our profession to get tied up in all sorts of practical and theoretical knots. Knots that not only make it difficult for us to understand and explain our role but have also stopped us from developing a better way of 'doing' our job.

In this book, I am going to recount for you what I learned on my voyage of discovery. I hope that this book will help unravel all that mess. In many ways, this book is a journal of my descent in project management despair before ascending back into the dawn of a new project management day. In this book, we will explore *why* the original project managers chose the theoretical roots of our profession and how these roots have ended up bearing some strange fruit.

This book will not cover the well-trodden paths of project management. If you want to know how to be better at planning, scheduling, and controlling a project, then this is probably not the book for you. But, if you want to know *why* project managers think they need to do these things and, even more controversially, explore if they even should, then you've come to the right place.

For my part, I think of this book as a joint venture. It's an opportunity for you and me to shine a light on project management and reveal some of our dirty little secrets. To investigate some of the glaring problems with the way project management sees itself and why this is creating a Dr. Jekyll/Mr. Hyde vibe in the profession. We will also explore some new ideas like the 'project management elephant', 'phenomenological value', 'the project eco-system', 'order-generating rules' and whether the 'experience of project management' is more important than delivering a 'successful project'. In the end, I hope these ideas will change the way you think about project management.

Now if all goes according to my cunning plan, this book will rock your world so much that it destroys, and then rebuilds, your understanding of project management. Anyway, that's the plan. So, grab a coffee, turn your mobile phone onto silent, change your outlook calendar to 'in a meeting' and let's get cracking.

In the Beginning

Long before anyone started describing themselves as 'project managers' things were getting done. Roads were built, pyramids were constructed, and entire empires were established. However, it wasn't until the start of the first Industrial Revolution and the birth of mechanised manufacturing that anyone began to worry about things like deadlines, delays, quality control, mass production and resource planning. Before this, anything that needed to be made was created by craftsman who used secret 'rules of thumb' to decide how long it would take to make something, how much material they needed, when the material would be needed and whether they had enough material 'out the back' to finish the job.

But the arrival of mechanised manufacturing changed all that. New production centres, called factories, started producing goods so quickly and accurately that concepts like the speed of production, wastage, deadlines, warehousing of materials and quality management became significant drivers in the cost of producing the final products.

It was in this time of social and economic upheaval that many of the foundational principles of modern-day project management were born, such as Taylor's theory of scientific management, Shewhart's theories of quality management and Ford's theories on production and consumption. Together these three theories would become the heart and soul of a burgeoning new idea called 'production management'. This idea is an important one on our journey because it is the original port from which we set sail.

Traditionally, project management has been categorised as a subset of production management [1, 2]. Understanding that our profession is categorised this way is critical to our voyage of discovery because it helps us to understand how we got many of the ideas, systems, methods, processes and tools that we use every day. Of, course the real question is, 'Is project management categorised correctly?'—but we'll get to that. Right now, let's start by looking at the three fundamental theories that underpin production management.

Taylorism: Scientific Management

Frederick Winslow Taylor (1856–1915) was a mechanical engineer who set out to overcome the deficiencies that he saw in the new-fangled 'factories' that kept popping up all over America. Taylor was an optimist who saw the fantastic potential of the manufacturing era. He believed that, managed correctly, mechanised manufacturing could herald a new age of prosperity for both managers and workers. His entire book 'The Principles of Scientific Management' [3] is premised on the belief that '…The principal object of management should be to secure the maximum prosperity for the employer, coupled with the maximum prosperity for each employee…'.

But Taylor was more than just an idealist, he was also an engineer. It wasn't enough for him to simply make sweeping statements about how mechanised manufacturing could increase the prosperity of management and workers—he set about proving it.

Frederick Taylor was a precise man. He took nothing for granted. He disliked 'rules of thumb', and he detested wastage and poor-quality work. He was also the epitome of the empirical scientist. He 'scienced' the crap out of everything. Just to give you one example, in his book he recounts how, over 26 years, he conducted and recorded 50,000 experiments to determine the best possible method for cutting metal on a lathe. *I know right—OMG!*

But it was this attention to detail and scientific rigour that provided him with the foundation for his theory of scientific management. A theory which even today, over a century later, is still the basis for understanding almost everything about production and manufacturing.

Taylor's theory of scientific management is founded on five basic principles:

1. The intended goal of all 'work' needs to be clearly defined and must not change.
2. All 'work' can be de-constructed into 'tasks' which can then be scientifically studied in detail.
3. From this study, a repeatable, non-varying, best-practice process can be developed to ensure the most efficient performance of that task.
4. The role of management is to develop and document this process and to train the workers in the process.
5. The role of workers is to execute that process without question and without trying to improve it.

Shewhartism: Statistical Quality Control

Around the same time as Taylor was working on his principles of scientific management, Walter Andrew Shewhart (1891–1967) was becoming increasingly frustrated by the amount of unnecessary wastage that he observed in the manufacturing process at the Western Electric Company, where he worked as a manager. He also noticed that there was a direct correlation between the speed of production and an increase in poor quality products. This correlation meant that even when the speed of production increased, it did not necessarily follow that the total output for a day increased. In fact, in some cases, the faster the rate of production, the less usable product was produced at the end of the day. So, along with Edward Deming and Joseph Juran, he set about developing a scientifically based system that would both reduce waste and improve quality outcomes.

The basic principles that Shewhart, Deming and Juran would eventually outline would go onto become the foundations for concepts such as total quality management, Six Sigma and lean manufacturing [4, 5]. These principles are:

1. All, less than optimal quality outcomes, are a result of either an 'assignable-cause' or a 'chance-cause'.

2. All 'assignable-cause' defects can be eliminated through a properly documented process and rigorous management oversight.
3. All production processes must be scientifically studied to determine the least number of steps required to ensure optimal efficiency.
4. Production quality is increased by reducing deviations from the scientifically determined process.
5. Every deviation from a scientifically determined process will result in a decreased economic outcome.

Fordism: The Science of Mass Production

Henry Ford (1863–1947) is best known for his creation of the Ford motor vehicle, and later the Ford Motor Company. But his contribution to the industrial world goes far beyond just building cars. Henry Ford's factories were simply the physical manifestation of his philosophy that mechanised manufacturing is, in fact, an entire socio-political system [6].

Ford's production philosophy drew heavily from the principles of Taylorism, and so in one respect, it could be argued that Fordism is simply an extension of the principles of scientific management. However, Ford went further than Taylor had ever envisaged. Ford took the idea of the de-constructing 'work' into 'tasks' and then used this as the basis for streamlining production on a scale never seen before. He also shifted the idea of tasks from production theory to economic theory by introducing the idea that the machinery and the worker could be viewed as a single economic unit. Using this idea, he went on to change the manufacturing world by focussing on cost minimisation rather than profit maximisation. By reducing all work to its smallest possible task, what we call 'employing reductionist techniques', Henry Ford created a manufacturing system in which even the most complex manufacturing tasks could now be undertaken by predominantly unskilled labour. This meant he didn't need to pay artisans, craftsman and engineers top dollar to be on the factory floor—he only needed a handful of them sitting in a design office while the cheap labourers worked on the production line on the factory floor [7].

Henry Ford also introduced the concept of the 'push' system into production theory. In a 'push' system, you can increase the output of the production plant simply by controlling the speed of input. If you need more units produced in a day, you simply feed more into the start of the system and demand that the rest of the system keep up. In other words, you push through production without asking if the downstream system is capable of handling the increase.

Ford was also obsessed with the concept of standardisation. His entire production system was predicated on doing exactly the same thing in exactly the same way so that exactly the same product could be delivered to exactly the same quality standard every single time. In this way, his thoughts were very similar to Shewhart. This process of standardisation allowed Ford to pioneer the concept of mass production [6].

Of course, the one piece that was missing in this process was making sure you produced something that people wanted to purchase. For Henry Ford, this was the easy part. If you are the manufacturer, you simply tell the customer what they can have. In arguably one of his most cited statements, Henry Ford was asked by a journalist if customers could select different colours for their vehicles. Ford simply replied, 'You can have any colour you want – as long as it's black' [8]. Under a Fordist-based production system, the manufacturer dictates both what went into the assembly system (standardised inputs) and what the consumer could have at the end (standardised outputs). Using this philosophy, Henry Ford was able to create arguably the most sophisticated production system of the age.

By combining these concepts, Henry Ford was able to produce some of the most technically complex machines of his time (the motor vehicle) using predominately unskilled labour, at a fraction of the cost of custom-built products and at the rate that he decided he wanted to make them.

Although Henry Ford borrowed a lot of his ideas from Taylor, he was able to expand on them to create a philosophy of manufacturing that would guide production management theory and practice for well over a century. The principles of this philosophy are simple:

1. Reductionist techniques can be used to deskill every task required in the process.
2. Inputs, processes and outputs must be standardised.
3. Increased output rate can be achieved by 'pushing' more into the system.
4. It's the manufacturer who decides what the output will be and how much it's worth.

Transformational Production Management

These three theories, Taylorism, Shewhartism and Fordism, became the foundation upon which a new model of management would be built. This new type of management was called 'production management', and it would become the body of theory from which 'project management' would ultimately evolve [9].

Production management can be conceptualised as a five-stage model. The transformation process starts with the manufacturer identifying a need in the marketplace. The manufacturer then determines what to make and acquires the necessary inputs (these will be a combination of materials, labour, time and knowledge). These inputs are put through a specific production process. This process *transforms* the inputs into the desired output. The manufacturer can then use this output to

Fig. 1.1 The 'transformational' production management system

satisfy the identified need in the marketplace. This 'transformational' production management model is shown in Fig. 1.1.

This model, or variants of it, is the basis of almost every manufacturing process outlined in production management textbooks. It is the foundation of cost analysis, unit pricing, factory layout and design, procurement, logistics and even sales and marketing. This simple, five-stage model is the foundation of the 'value chain' which became a foundational model for modern-day project management.

Project Management

The specific date when the profession of project management began is a matter of dispute. Some argue that project management methods were practiced in the chemical production plants as early as World War II. Other authors argue that the works of Henri Fayol back in 1916 were the birthplace of project management [10]. Who knows? Or more precisely, who cares? Either way, the first documented evidence we have of modern-day project management processes being applied is in the early 1950s when the United States Navy started using systematic methods and processes to plan and deliver the 'Polaris Missile' project.

This new idea of 'managing' projects seemed to work so well, that NASA, the US Department of Defence, large engineering companies and construction firms all started to take notice. Once these industry movers and shakers jumped on the project management wagon, there was no turning back—the age of project management arrived. In the 1980s, project management methodologies were quickly being adapted for a new industry—computer and software manufacturing. This new industry moved a lot quicker than the traditional manufacturing or construction processes, so new ways of 'doing' project management were developed. However, these new ways are essentially grounded on the same basic theories of production. Sure, they move through the cycles faster, but the foundational principles were always the same.

After that, everyone seemed to get on board the project management wagon. Formal training programs were developed, registration and certification programs sprang up, universities developed courses and project management became a profession [11].

In the grand scheme of things, the development of the project management profession has been lightning fast. Other professions such as the medical, legal and accounting professions have taken centuries to develop and document their grounding theories. By these standards, project management is still in its infancy. As a profession, we went from not even existing to being responsible for the largest and most complex activities on the planet in less than three decades. This rate of growth was possible because our predecessors simply grabbed the theory of 'production management' and said 'That's close enough, let's go!'

However, they were also savvy enough to see that what they were doing was not exactly 'production management'. So how did they go about explaining how project management was different to production management? Well, they focused on two key ideas that delineated project management from production management:

1. Projects have a defined lifespan (i.e. they are not operations).
2. Projects create unique outputs (i.e. they can't be mass-produced).

These two ideas seemed sufficiently different from what was being done in the manufacturing world to justify the need for a different type of management. So, to demonstrate that project management was different to production management, our predecessors created a definition for projects, that went like this:

> A project is a temporary endeavour undertaken to create a unique product, service or result... [1]

At this juncture, it's important to understand what just happened. Rather than sitting down and really thinking about what project management is, our professional forebears began by defining what the profession was not. In other words, '…although we might look like production management, we aren't'.

Now, don't get me wrong. That is not a criticism. In fact, it was precisely because our predecessors were able to grab an 'off-the-shelf' solution in terms of theoretical foundations that our profession got off to such a sprint at the start. What's more, it's because those theoretical foundations seemed to work so well for us that our profession has gone from strength to strength in the decades that followed.

However, grabbing the nearest theory and using that as the foundation of our profession brought with it some systemic flaws. Flaws that are only now becoming apparent as the profession begins to mature. These flaws stem from some of the foundational assumptions within production management theory that look right when you glance at them, but simply don't stand up under more rigorous scrutiny. These flaws have tainted our view of project management and, in my opinion, are hindering us from developing the new systems, processes, and tools we need to excel in our roles.

But hey, don't just take my word for it. Let's navigate through these dark waters together.

Slaughtering Sacred Cows

Now before we lift the hood and start tinkering with the engine of project management, I want to go through a bit of neuroscience with you. Specifically, the concept of *perception*.

In technical terms, perception is the identification and interpretation of stimuli based on our memory. To perceive anything, we need to go through three steps. These are:

1. Selecting the stimuli we want to see by filtering out the bits we don't want to see.

2. Organising our selected stimuli into patterns that are familiar to us.
3. Interpreting those patterns so that we have a 'logical' foundation for our subsequent actions.

Perception allows our minds to absorb vast amounts of information and make sense of it [12]. This process has served humans well and has allowed us to evolve into the dominant species on the planet. However, the process of perception has a dark side. If the 'sense' we make from the information is incorrect, we may find ourselves consistently making poor choices—and worse yet, failing to even understand why these choices are wrong.

One way to demonstrate how perception can change your understanding of the world is to introduce you to the concept of Lazarus species. Lazarus species are groups of animals that humans believed were extinct, only to find out decades later that they were not. The New Zealand storm petrel is one example of this.

The New Zealand storm petrel is a small seabird that was classified as extinct in 1850. Since then, archaeologists have speculated about the petrel. Photographs of the skins of the petrel were displayed in museums. Academics wrote papers on historical migration patterns, food sources and generally any aspect of the petrel's existence that they could glean from the small amount of empirical evidence at hand.

But then on 25 January 2003, things got...*awkward*. A fisherman off the Coromandel Peninsula in New Zealand's North Island managed to capture photographs of three 'extinct' birds as they flew around his charter boat trying to steal his catch [13].

Well, overnight everything in the ornithological world changed. Instead of archaeologist being interested in petrels, biologists were. Rather than spending money on research grants to document the history of the petrel, the New Zealand government gave grants to conservationists to study and protect the petrel. As a result, between 2005 and 2009, a dedicated capture program resulted in not only finding the island where these birds breed but also managing to capture another 11 of these 'extinct' birds for study purposes.

This is why perception can get you into trouble. Regardless of how extinct ornithologist perceived the petrel to be, the simple fact was that they were totally and utterly wrong. But their *perception* dictated how they *behaved* towards the petrel. The poor petrel didn't even know it was supposed to be extinct. It just went about doing what it does, living its life, completely unaware how many research papers, study grants and museum displays were dedicated in its honour.

But when new information came to light, the whole 'petrel world' was turned upside down. Now here's the most important bit—*the facts hadn't changed at all*. It's not like the petrel willed itself back from extinction. The only thing that changed was people's perception about the petrel, and that shift in perception changed everything.

So, as I said earlier, the dark side of perception is that we can be totally convinced by what we believe to be true even though it's completely wrong. This perception of being 'right' causes us to say and do things that we think are 100%

rational and sane but are just plain wrong…and unfortunately, that's not the worst of it.

Remember I said that the first step in perception is selecting the stimuli we want to see, by filtering out the bits we don't want to see? That's a documented phenomenon called *confirmation bias*. Confirmation bias means that once we have gone to the effort of filtering and sorting the stimuli in our world, we generally don't keep doing it. Filtering out the vast number of stimuli in our world is hard, so our brains find ways not to have to keep doing it. The easiest way is to only see facts that reinforce what we already believe to be true and ignoring information that might be contradictory to what we already believe.

Now I know what you are thinking, 'Blah, blah, blah…What has any of this got to do with project management?'

Great question!

But before I answer it, let me ask you this. If I could show you some glaring holes in your perception of project management, would you be willing to have your world turned upside down, or would you prefer not to know?

Time to pick the red pill or the blue pill, Neo.

Lifting the Hood

Oh, good—you stayed. That's encouraging.

We have already discussed that the foundational theory of project management comes from production management. Almost all the methodologies, systems, tools and practices that we employ in the daily execution of our role can be traced back to either Taylorism, Shewhartism or Fordism. The Iron Triangle, CPM/PERT scheduling, WBS, quality management and a whole range of other concepts, tools and systems all come from these theories. In fact, every single one of the 47 project management processes outlined in the PMBoK [1] has a direct link to one of these three theories.

So, let's start our 'perception check' by having a look at some of the assumptions which underpin these theories.

Taylorism

The first principle of Taylorism has to do with the reason *why* the work is being done. Taylor's first principle is that all work needs to be clearly defined before you start production and that the goal of the work must not change. Now, I think we can all agree that getting the scope definition right at the start of any project is critical, but it's the whole idea that the thing is then set in stone that I have trouble with. *In theory*, the idea that the project's stated raison d'être never changes 'sounds' reasonable, but my experience over the last 20 years is that the stated goal of the project is **never** set in stone.

To demonstrate, let me give you a 'hypothetical' example. Let's say you have spent the last 12 months working with a group of stakeholders as they defined and documented the new hospital that they need to build. They agree that it needs to have 400 beds, a maternity ward and an oncology department. You get the brief and design signed off, schedule out the project, start procuring the contractors and suppliers and finally get underway on site. You are, hypothetically of course, 5 months, 3 weeks and 2 days into the construction. The sub-footings and foundations are poured, the structural columns well underway and you are finalising design details for the post-tensioned slab. Then the Sponsor comes to a Project Control Group meeting and says, 'Our funding has been cut. We can now only afford 360 beds and we need to lose the maternity ward. We also need to build five specialist consultant suites so we can rent these out'.

What would you do?

Obviously, based on Taylor's first principle, you would just turn around and say, 'Look, I'm sorry, but we agreed upfront what this project was going to deliver. See, here is your signature on this document' (at this point you could even wave the document around a little to prove your point), and then you'd say 'So, I'm afraid that the "clearly defined" goal of this project simply cannot change. This project will be delivering 400 beds, a maternity ward and the oncology department exactly as we agreed, and I thank you for your understanding'.

Yeah, right!

What really happens? We just roll with the punches, we think outside the box, we adapt and we overcome. If you have ever been in a situation like this, then maybe you can agree with me that Taylor's assumption that the goal of a project must not change once it has been clearly defined and documented is a little… how do I put this nicely? Off the mark.

Taylor's second principle is that all work can be deconstructed into tasks, and these tasks can be studied in detail. In project management, we use this principle to develop our WBS, activity lists and project schedules. So, there is no doubt that a large part of our role is taking the complexity of 'work' and breaking it down into manageable 'tasks' that can be assigned to others. But I can't help but think there is something 'off' with the assumption that everything a project manager does can be broken down into tasks that can be studied in detail.

The unique nature of projects dictates an element of uncertainty. Of course, we plan out everything we can, but in the immortal words of Donald Rumsfeld '…we know, there are known knowns; there are things we know we know. We also know there are known unknowns; that is to say, we know there are some things we do not know. But there are also unknown unknowns—the ones we don't know we don't know. … It is the latter category that tends to be the difficult ones'.

In my experience there are tasks involved in the delivery of projects that aren't planned for, they just 'pop-up'. Now, maybe I'm doing it wrong, but when these sorts of things come up, I don't say 'Listen, I need to break this new work down into individual tasks and study it in detail before I can help you resolve it'. No, I just get in and do it. Now, if you find that your role requires you to do things like this—things that are unplanned and have a level of complexity that can't be deconstructed and studied in detail before you have to resolve them—then you too might feel that there is something 'off' about the assumptions that underpin Taylor's second principle.

Taylor's third principle is that any task that has been sufficiently de-constructed can be developed into a repeatable, non-varying, best-practice process to ensure the most efficient performance of that task. I might have missed something here, but doesn't the definition of a project contain the word 'unique'? Can anyone explain to me how something unique can be delivered using a repeatable, non-varying, best-practice process? Doesn't the very nature of 'unique' mean that it's not repeatable, that the next one will vary and that it's only done once? But Taylor's third principle relies on the ability to repeat a task as many times as necessary to work out the best practice. It also requires both the ability to control all the variables in the process and a stable and unchanging production environment in which to conduct your scientific experiments. Last time I checked a project manager gets none of these luxuries.

Taylor's fourth principle is that it is the role of management to develop and document the process and then to train the workers in the process. Keep in mind that when Taylor talks about developing and documenting the process, he is not talking about a general framework for delivering projects like the one we have in PMBoK®. This is the guy who conducted over 50,000 experiments into the most efficient way to cut a specific type of metal. So, when Taylor is talking about developing and documenting the process, he means doing it in so much detail that nothing is left unexplained and nothing is left to chance.

If you subscribe to Taylor's fourth principle, then your next project start-up meeting should go something like this:

> *We are going to start the project on Monday, I'd like to spend the first five or so years doing a few thousand experiments on the most effective way to complete each task in the project so that I can document it in detail and then train all my staff in exactly how it needs to be done so that we can really maximise our efficiency. Is everyone OK with that?... no, I can't just do what I did on the last project, they are all unique you know. <eye-roll>*

Again, we see the assumptions that projects do not have any time constraints and that they are delivered in an environment that can be sufficiently controlled to allow the testing and retesting of every task in the process. But as you and I both know, this never happens in projects.

Taylor's final principle is that the role of the workers is to execute the process that management has developed without question and without trying to improve it. Do I even need to walk you through this one? If I didn't listen to suggestions from my team, I'd be dead in the water. The uniqueness of projects demands a certain level of collaborative problem-solving. Just because I had a workable solution on the last project, it doesn't mean that it will work on the next one. In my experience, I've found that I need every head in the game—all the time. I want everyone involved in the project looking for risks and opportunities, identifying better solutions and generally getting the best possible outcome using the least amount of resources.

Basically, what I'm saying is that I want the people involved in the project to do **the exact opposite** of Taylor's fifth principle.

Ok, so maybe project management has one or two *minor challenges* with the assumptions that we have adopted from Taylorism. Maybe things will get better when we look at quality management.

Shewhartism

Shewhart's first principle is that any less than optimal outcomes are a result of either an 'assignable-cause' or a 'chance-cause'. In layperson's terms, Shewhart is saying that quality issues result from either something that we can control or something that we can't. This is a reasonable enough assessment of the world, so I think we can happily adopt this principle into project management theory.

Shewhart's second principle is where things start to get wobbly. Shewhart's second principle is that *all* 'assignable-cause' defects can be eliminated through a properly documented process and rigorous management oversight. Now we have already explored the issues that arise on projects when it comes to the idea of 'properly documenting' a process. But I do think there is a need for project managers to learn from their experience and to ensure that these lessons are communicated to others in the project team. The premise of the project management lesson learnt process is borne from Shewhart's idea of elimination through documentation. The problem is the 'unique' aspect of projects which ensures that even though I might have had a similar situation on another project, I may need to do things a little differently this time. This means that a project manager can't just 'read and execute the documented process'. Instead, the project manager needs to apply abductive reasoning to see how the lessons learnt from past projects can be applied to a new project. This is not the same thing as Shewhart's principle—in fact, it is something quite different. Shewhart's principle requires unwavering application of a documented process, while abductive reasoning requires creative problem-solving using the documented process. So, for now, let's just say I 'kind-of' agree with Shewhart on this one.

Next is the issue of eliminating quality defects through the process of rigorous management oversight. Again, this sounds like we could agree on, but I still have some nagging doubts. Maybe we should take a closer look.

The idea of management oversight is the reason why our profession exists. Everyone agrees that projects are too unwieldy to simply be left to chance. We are brought in to 'oversee' the project by guiding the process. But the idea of eliminating quality defects through management oversight requires a few critical assumptions. One is that we have the ability to observe all aspects of the 'production process' for long enough and in enough detail, that we will be able to identify any deviations from the documented process. Two, it assumes that we can sufficiently control the production environment so that the cause of the defect is removed from the process 'next time' we do it. Three, it assumes there is sufficient repetition of output to justify the cost and time necessary to identify the 'assignable-cause' and then rectify the process. Now, while there are elements of these assumptions that are correct in the practice of project management, there are also large chunks that aren't. So, once again, I'm going to suggest that the jury is still out on whether this is the right theory for project management.

Shewhart's third principle is that all production process must be studied to determine the least number of steps required to ensure optimal efficiency. Nope, we've been through this one. Not going to happen. The unique nature of projects hinders the level of detailed scientific study required to determine the least number of steps. The temporary nature of a project does not provide the cost/time benefit to do the study, and the dynamic nature of the project environment thwarts the idea that we can somehow stick to the documented procedure. Sorry, Walter—this one is out.

Shewhart's final principle is that production quality is increased by reducing deviations from the scientifically determined process. Can I say that, in principle, I agree 100% with Shewhart's assumptions here, and *if* projects had a scientifically determined process for standardised delivery… well, then they wouldn't be projects; they would be operations. Once again we get snookered by the idea that projects are unique. You can't have an outcome that is both unique and standardised. They are mutually exclusive concepts. So, in terms of project management theory, this one is off the table.

Fordism

Fordism is a philosophy of mass production, not unique outputs (*I think you can already see where I'm headed with this one, but we've given Taylorism and Shewhartism a work-over, so let's round it out with Fordism*).

Ford's first principle is to use reductionist techniques to deskill every task required in the process. If we apply this to project management, this means you—the project manager—would need to de-construct the project to the point where you could just walk out on the street, grab the first person you see and say, 'Do that. You don't need any prior knowledge or understanding of what we need to achieve. Just do the simple repetitive task exactly as I showed you—nothing more, nothing less'. Once again, this is totally inconceivable in the project management world. We have neither the time to do this nor would it make economic sense.

Ford's second principle is that you can increase the production rate by 'pushing' more into the production system. This is so wrong, I literally don't even know where to start. I just have a vision of a concreter punching me in the face because I said 'I've decided you aren't going fast enough, so I've ordered twice as much concrete for tomorrow. Make sure you get it poured'. Dictating the rate of output is not simply a matter of whether there are enough resources available at the time we need them; you also need to factor in the element of uncertainty inherent in the delivery environment. Projects will never have the level of control necessary to dictate the required rate of output.

Ford's third principle is that the manufacturer decides what the consumer will get and therefore gets to determine the value of that product. So, let me get this one straight; basically, the project manager turns up to the stakeholders and says, 'I've decided that you need a [fill in the blank]. Now, I've taken the liberty of constructing one for you and here is the bill. I take cash, cheque or credit card—how would you like to pay?'

Look, I suspect that this can happen depending on the size and nature of the project, but in my experience over the last 20 years, that's not how it goes. Generally, the stakeholders come to me with what they *think they want*. Then I work with them to find out what *they really need*. After that, we all hope that what *actually gets delivered* is close to what we all agreed on upfront. So, I think it's safe to say, this last principle is out as well.

Now sit up straight, it's time for a quick quiz. I've gathered together all the underlying assumptions of production management, and I want you to decide if these align with your own experiences of project management. You can choose 'yes' if it aligns and 'no' if it doesn't. I've also given you a column for 'kind of' in case you think it sought of fits your experience, but still has some gaps.

Assumption	Yes	No	Kind of
The intended goal of all 'work' needs to be clearly defined and must not change			
All 'work' can be de-constructed into 'tasks' which can then be scientifically studied in detail			
From this study, a repeatable, non-varying, best-practice process can be developed to ensure the most efficient performance of that task			
The role of management is to develop and document this process and to train the 'workers' in the process			
The role of 'workers' is to execute that process without question and without trying to 'improve' the process			
All, less than optimal quality outcomes, are a result of either an 'assignable-cause' or a 'chance-cause'			
All 'assignable-cause' defects can be eliminated through a properly documented process and rigorous management oversight			
All production processes must be scientifically studied to determine the least number of steps required to ensure optimal efficiency			
Production quality is increased by reducing deviations from the scientifically determined process			
Every deviation from a scientifically determined process will result in a decreased economic outcome			
Reductionist techniques can be used to deskill every task required in the process			
Inputs, processes and outputs can be standardised			
Increased production rate can be achieved by 'pushing' more into the production system			
The manufacturer decides what the output will be and how much it's worth			
Totals			

How did you go? I would expect that if these assumptions were a good foundation for our profession, then you would be averaging about 80–90% in the 'yes' column. Is that what you got? Personally, I got 7% in the 'yes' column, 78% in the 'no' column and 15% in the 'kind of' column.

Hello! That's over 90% of the underlying assumptions of the production management theory that don't align with my experience of project management.

That can't be right, can it? Or maybe it is, and there is something fundamentally wrong here.

Pardon Me but Your Hard Paradigm Is Showing

Many researchers and authors have bemoaned the shortcomings of production management theory when it is applied to project management practice. However, by far the loudest voices are all crying out about the same problem, 'What about the people?'

Production management theory is all based on what is called the 'hard paradigm', which is just another way of saying that production management theory is 100% focused on the delivery of a product. There is no consideration in production management theory for 'human factors'. The only mention of 'humans' in production management theory is either in terms of identifying or satisfying customer's needs or whether a person should be categorised as a 'thinker' (management) or a 'doer' (worker).

For those of us who deliver projects, we know that 'people' have a constant and active role in the delivery of projects. As Pant and Baroudi [14] argue, '…managing relationships are critical through all stages of the project…'. There is a human side to project management that is either ignored or, at the very least, significantly underrepresented in the production management theory.

What's missing from the production management theory are 'soft skills'. These are the social skills that project managers need to deliver their projects, such as leadership, communication, decision-making, creativity, problem-solving, team building, emotional intelligence, conflict resolution, consensus building, etc.

The omission of 'soft skills' from production management theory is another one of the systemic flaws associated with our initial 'grab and go' approach to the project management body of theory. In the years that have followed our emergence as a profession, more and more researchers and practitioners have become convinced that these soft skills are not just 'another thing' that project managers should be doing. They could, in fact, be the most important thing project manager's do.

But the problem is, where does this fit into project management theory?

…and how about that definition?

Now, while I'm here butchering project management sacred cows, I guess I may as well commit the ultimate heresy and say that I also have a real problem with the current definition of projects. Here's why. PMBoK[(R)] [1] defines a project as '…a temporary endeavour undertaken to create a unique product, service or result…' (p. 5).

The idea of 'temporary' was included in the definition of projects to delineate them from operations [2, 9]. PMBoK® [1] then explains that '…temporary means that [a] project has a definite beginning and a definite end…temporary does not necessarily mean short in duration…' (p. 5). However, since every activity in human history has a definite beginning and has, or will have, a definite end, how then can 'temporary' be used to identify what is a project and what is not?

The use of the term 'short' is also problematic. It is both ambiguous and subjective. On one end of the known timescale, we have the shortest amount of time measurable, which is the time it takes for light to travel one Planck length in a vacuum $(5.39 \times 10^{-44}$ s). On the other end of the timescale, we know that the entire duration that human beings have been on earth can be considered 'short' by cosmological standards. So, exactly what is the timescale that should be used when deciding the correct length of *shortness* necessary to delineate a project from other activities?

Next, we have the problem of uniqueness. By nominating 'uniqueness' as a defining attribute of a project's outcome, PMBoK® has ostensibly funnelled any and every human activity into the definition. Using 'uniqueness' as a defining characteristic of projects means that a project could be anything from sending an email to a colleague, through to the evolution of the human species itself. Both could be considered to have 'unique' outcomes. Furthermore, and at the risk of adding irony to definitional challenges, if 'uniqueness' is a critical factor in defining a project, would it not stand to reason that if I was attempting to manufacture 100,000 widgets in a factory and 10 of those were not compliant with the specification, then the non-complaint (i.e. unique) widgets are, in fact, an accidental project in their own right?

What Does All This Mean?

Already in our short time together, we have managed to identify a range of potential problems associated with both the underlying principles of production management and the current definition of projects. I hope by now you are starting to arrive at the same conclusion that I did—production management theory doesn't seem to 'fit' what we do as project managers. On the surface, it looks like it does, but when you look under the hood, things simply aren't right. There are contradictions, gaps in the logic and entire class of fundamental skills totally omitted from our theory.

The basic problem is that the nature of projects runs contrary to almost all the foundational principles of production management theory. As a result, we find ourselves in a position where our current theoretical foundations are too formulaic [15], too reliant on hard paradigms and reductionist techniques [16–19], too linear in their approach [20], cannot deal with the dynamism and complexity of project work [21–23], provide no representation for soft skills [24–26] and fail to represent the totality of the lived experience of project management [8, 28].

Because of these deficiencies, project management researchers keep trying to 'bolt on' other bodies of theory to plug the holes. We have researchers suggesting that we should replace production management theory with either strategic management theory, complexity theory, TFV (time-flow-value) theory or paradox theory [19, 28–32]. At the same time, we have other authors arguing that we can't simply abandon production management theory because so many of the tools we need are all grounded in it [33].

As I read through the arguments from both sides of the project management debate, I found myself agreeing with both arguments and yet, at the same time, thinking 'yes, but…' to most of the subsequent findings. It's taken me a while to understand how both sides of the debate can be both kind of right and simultaneously not right at all. But I eventually worked it out.

Elephants!

The Elephant

There's a poem by John G. Saxby which helps us understand the danger of experience and how this can cloud our ability to understand our world. This poem is called 'The Blind Men and the Elephant', and it goes like this:

> It was six men of Indostan, to learning much inclined, who went to see the elephant (Though all of them were blind). That each by observation, might satisfy his mind.

> The first approached the elephant, and happening to fall against its broad and sturdy side, at once began to bawl: "God bless me! but the elephant is nothing but a wall!"

> The second feeling of the tusk cried, "Ho! what have we here? So very round and smooth and sharp? To me 'tis mighty clear. This wonder of an elephant is very like a spear!"

> The third approached the animal and, happening to take the squirming trunk within his hands," I see," quoth he, "The elephant is very like a snake!"

> The fourth reached out his eager hand and felt about the knee. "What most this wondrous beast is like, is mighty plain" quoth he "Tis clear enough the elephant is very like a tree."

> The fifth, who chanced to touch the ear, said "E'en the blindest man can tell what this resembles most. Deny the fact who can, this marvel of an elephant, is very like a fan!"

> The sixth no sooner had begun about the beast to grope, than seizing on the swinging tail, that fell within his scope. "I see," quoth he, "the elephant is very like a rope!"

> And so, these men of Indostan, disputed loud and long. Each in his own opinion, exceeding stiff and strong. Though each was partly in the right, and all were in the wrong.

> So, oft in philosophic wars, the disputants I ween, tread on in utter ignorance of what each other mean, and prate about the elephant not one of them has seen!

This poem highlights the danger of experience and perception. Once each of the blind men had 'experienced' the elephant, they were one hundred per cent sure what the elephant was. Based on their own *very real but extremely limited* perception of the elephant, they began arguing about what the elephant looked like. None of them could convince the others to accept their description. But neither were any of them willing to be convinced that their description was wrong. The reason they couldn't reach an agreement is that each of their experiences, and therefore their perceptions, of the elephant is different.

Despite all of them now having experienced an elephant, their limited perception only meant they could not, individually, comprehend or explain to the others what an elephant is. So, although in one respect, they were now wiser about what an elephant is, they are, at the same time, no closer to comprehending it than they were when they stood in ignorance.

Project management is the same.

Because the definition of projects is so expansive and inclusive, each of us can experience project management completely differently from one another. This doesn't mean that any of the different experiences are wrong, just that none of them provides the full picture.

So, the light bulb moment for me in my journey was realising that we need to stop trying 'correct' other project managers' perception of the profession, based on our own experience, and instead open our minds to the idea that we might actually all be right, even though it is different for all of us.

I believe that if we want to get a better understanding of what project management really is, we need to step back from our little part of the project management elephant, perceive project management more holistically and, then, collaboratively create a new understanding of what project management is. We don't throw away production management theory, because it doesn't quite fit into our experience. Instead, we ask 'Is this part of something bigger? Am I only holding an ear here? And if so, what does the rest of this mighty beast look like?'

The Value Problem

Earlier I introduced you to the five-stage, transformational production management model. This model steps through the process of need identification, input acquisition, transformation, outputs creation and need satisfaction. This linear process is typical of the way the production management world sees the creation of value. It's a value chain. Each step in the process adds something new to the product being developed.

This perspective assumes that value is *inherent in the product*. In other words, if at any point the production process was to stop, it would be possible to determine the exact value of the product. This would be equal to the cost of all the materials, labour and time used to create the product, plus some margin of profit for the producer. Viola, easy.

Now, this perspective of value is what Adam Smith, the father of modern economics, called 'exchange value' [34]. Basically, the value of the product is equivalent to whatever another person is willing to exchange for that thing. That exchange could be another commodity, like in a bartering system, but most often the equivalency is decided by the exchange of money. This is the concept of value that most people would be familiar with, but it's not the only concept of value that exists. For example, in Hegelian philosophy, the concept of value is phenomenological—which is just a fancy way of saying it is created through experiences.

One of the problems that I encountered when I started exploring the concept of creating value in the project management space is that the English language uses words like cost, worth and value interchangeably. This brought me back to the problem of trying to 'describe the elephant'. If we are all holding different parts of the animal but only have a single term to describe it, we can't differentiate our experiences to see how it all might fit together. The trunk is an elephant, the leg is an elephant, and the ear is an elephant.

To overcome this problem, I'm going to separate the terms cost, worth and value like this: '*Cost*' is the combination of materials, labour and time necessary to create a physical product. '*Worth*' is what someone else is willing to exchange for that product. '*Value*' is the feelings that a person attaches to that product.

Confused? Here, I'll give you an example.

Let's say a jeweller decides to make a gold ring. The *cost* of the materials, labour and time to make that ring are empirically quantifiable. For argument's sake, let's say its $300.00. Once the jeweller has made the ring, she attempts to exchange that ring for money, and she hopes that someone in the market thinks the ring is **worth** $1000.00. For the sake of our story, let's assume a young man agrees with the jeweller and exchanges $1000.00 for the ring. The next day, that young man gives the ring to the woman he loves and asks her to marry him. The woman accepts both his proposal and the ring.

The following day you go to that woman and say, 'I'll give you $1,200.00 for your new ring'. What do you think the chances would be that she would sell the ring to you? I'm guessing slim to none. Why? Because for her, the **value** of the ring can no longer be measured in terms of monetary exchange. Something intangible has happened—the **value** of the ring has eclipsed both what the ring **cost** and what it is **worth**.

Now when I talk about 'value', 'creating value' or 'value-adding' throughout the rest of this book, I'm talking about this phenomenological idea of value. I'm talking about an intangible attribute that a person attaches to the experience of being involved with your project.

This definition of value creates interesting challenges and opportunities for project managers. These primarily have to do with the subjective nature of value and the emotional connections that create it.

In the phenomenological definition, 'value' is subjective. Establishing the value of your project is an intensely personal experience. Some of the people involved with the project will *value* the sense of pride they get from delivering a project on time and under budget. Others might *value* the sense of accomplishment they get from achieving something which is outside their comfort zone. Still others might *value* the sense of camaraderie that they gain from working side by side with their brothers and sisters in arms as they navigate through some challenging times. There really is no way for you to know exactly what will generate value for the individuals involved in your project.

This means that every single person involved with the project will have a different opinion of whether the project is creating value for them. While this can create challenges for you as the project manager, it also presents opportunities. In particular, it means you can 'create' value by skillfully managing the experiences of those involved.

Phenomenologically based value is emotionally driven. This provides an opportunity for a skilled project manager to decouple traditional project 'success' or 'failure', from the experience of delivering the project [35–38]. Decoupling empirically assessable criteria from an emotional response can be an incredibly powerful tool for the project manager, particularly if your project seems to be going off the rails. Separating people's emotional experience from empirical criteria such as 'on time' and 'under budget' gives a skilled project manager the opportunity to create value for the people involved, even if the project is labelled a failure by empirical standards. Don't worry, I will cover this in a lot more detail in Section 'The Experience', but for now let me just put this out there: *You don't need to bring your project in under budget and on time for people to get value from your project.*

Another challenge/opportunity presented by the phenomenological definition of value is that it is not easily controlled. It can take on a life of its own. Delivering projects requires networks of people to work together for a set time to deliver a common goal. A network is made up of nodes (in this case, people) and connections (the relationships between those people) [39]. Often, these networks rely on other networks to be able to achieve their own tasks and goals. This creates an intricate web of interconnecting and emotionally volatile social interactions. The complexity that these social connections create in your project is the subject of future sections, but for now, let's just say these social interactions create an opportunity for *value co-creation*.

Value co-creation requires everyone involved in the project to become less 'product-centric'. It requires them to think more strategically and holistically about the wider context of 'why' the project is being undertaken and then using that knowledge to create a framework to guide the project towards the desired outcome. Winter and Szczepanek [40] argue that the concept of value co-creation is particularly relevant for projects because projects need to create mutual benefits not only for everyone involved with the projects but also for their extended networks.

In simple terms, value co-creation occurs through the dynamic interface of three separate components: (1) the people; (2) the environment; and (3) the project [41]. In terms of project management, value is 'co-created' through the social interactions that occur whenever these three components overlap, and it can happen in the most unusual ways. Value can be generated when people face challenges together or when they have a shared vision; when they have to solve problems as a team; and, if managed well, even when there is conflict. All of these have a role to play in creating value in projects. The concept of co-creating value in a project also highlights that no one person can 'create' value on their own. It's the connections with the other people that creates the value.

In my opinion, the concept of value co-creation is the main reason why traditional production management fails to align with the lived experience of project management. Social interactions don't fall neatly into any of the underlying assumptions of production management. However, they consume large amounts of a project manager's time and energy. What's more, the idea of value co-creation means that a project's value can be greater than the sum of its parts. It's not enough to simply break down work into tasks and then schedule these in the correct order. There is something else going on. Something 'outside' the project.

So, let's see if we can work out what 'something else' is.

References

1. Project Management Institute (U.S.) (2017) A guide to the project management body of knowledge (PMBOK® Guide), 6th edn. Project Management Institute, Newtown Square, PA
2. Koskela L, Ballard G (2006) Should project management be based on theories of economics or production? Build Res Inform 34(2):154–163
3. Taylor FW (1911) The principles of scientific management. Harper & Brothers, New York, NY
4. Deming WE (1967) Walter A. Shewhart, 1891-1967. Am Stat 21(2):39–40
5. Shewhart WA (1931) Economic control of quality of manufactured product. ASQ Quality Press
6. Naruse T (1991) Taylorism and Fordism in Japan. Int J Polit Econ:32–48

7. Bak R (2003) Henry and Edsel: the creation of the ford empire. Wiley, Hoboken, NJ
8. Gelderman CW (1981) Henry Ford: the wayward capitalist. Dial Press, New York
9. Koskela L, Howell G (2008) The underlying theory of project management is obsolete. Eng Manage Rev IEEE 36(2):22–34
10. Fayol H (1916) General principles of management. Class Organizat Theory 2(15):57–69
11. Kwak YH, Anbari FT (2009) Analyzing project management research: perspectives from top management journals. Int J Proj Manag 27(5):435–446
12. Weick KE, Sutcliffe KM, Obstfeld D (2005) Organizing and the process of sensemaking. Organ Sci 16(4):409–421
13. Flood B (2003) The New Zealand storm-petrel is not extinct. Bird World 16(11):479–482
14. Pant I, Baroudi B (2008) Project management education: the human skills imperative. Int J Proj Manag 26(2):124–128
15. Wellman JL (2011) Improving project performance: eight habits of successful project teams. Macmillan
16. Usher G (2019) Creating confidence amongst complexity: the 'lived experience' of client-side project managers in the Australian construction sector. Ph.D., Business and Management, University of Southern Queensland, Brisbane, Australia
17. Usher G, Whitty SJ (2017) Identifying and managing drift-changes. Int J Proj Manag 35(4):586–603
18. Usher G, Whitty SJ (2017) Project Management Yinyang: coupling project success and client satisfaction. Proj Manage Res Pract 4
19. Usher G, Whitty SJ (2017) Embracing Paradox: utilizing design thinking in project management. In: Innovate, influence and implement—proceedings of the australian institute of project management national conference, Melbourne
20. Thomas J, Mengel T (2008) Preparing project managers to deal with complexity—advanced project management education. Int J Proj Manag 26(3):304–315
21. Aritua B, Smith NJ, Bower D (2009) Construction client multi-projects—a complex adaptive systems perspective. Int J Proj Manag 27(1):72–79
22. Bakhshi J, Ireland V, Gorod A (2016) Clarifying the project complexity construct: past, present and future. Int J Proj Manag 34(7):1199–1213
23. Usher G, Whitty SJ (2017) The final state convergence model. Int J Manag Proj Bus 10(4):770–795
24. Adams H (2016) A different approach to project management: the use of soft skills. http://digitalcommons.harrisburgu.edu/pmgt_dandt/2
25. Gillard S (2009) Soft skills and technical expertise of effective project managers. Issues Inform Sci Inf Technol 6
26. Mahasneh KJ, Thabet W (2015) Rethinking construction curriculum: a descriptive cause analysis for the soft skills gap among construction graduates. In: 51st ASC Annual International Conference Proceedings
27. Marando A (2012) Balancing project management hard skills and soft skills. http://projectmgmt.brandeis.edu/downloads/BRU_MSMPP_WP_Feb2012_Balancing_project_Management.pdf
28. Cicmil S, Williams T, Thomas J, Hodgson D (2006) Rethinking Project Management: researching the actuality of projects. Int J Proj Manag 24(8):675–686
29. Usher G (2014) Rethinking project management theory: a case for a paradigm shift in the foundational theory of client-side, construction, project management. Presented at the proceedings of the Australian Institute of Project Management National Conference, Brisbane
30. Cicmil S, Cooke-Davies T, Crawford L, Richardson K (2017) Exploring the complexity of projects: implications of complexity theory for project management practice. Project Management Institute
31. Cooke-Davies T, Cicmil S, Crawford L, Richardson K (2007) We're not in Kansas anymore, Toto: mapping the strange landscape of complexity theory, and its relationship to project management. Proj Manag J 38(2):50–61

32. Koskela L, Rooke J, Bertelsen S, Henrich G (2007) The TFV theory of production: new developments. Michigan: anais IGLC-15 International Group for Lean Construction
33. Winter M, Szczepanek T (2007) Reframing project management: new thinking, new practice. Gower, Farnham, England
34. Smith A (1950) An inquiry into the nature and causes of the Wealth of Nations,(1776). Methuen
35. Matinheikki J, Artto K, Peltokorpi A, Rajala R (2016) Managing inter-organizational networks for value creation in the front-end of projects. Int J Proj Manag 34(7):1226–1241
36. Matinheikki J, Pesonen T, Artto K, Peltokorpi A (2017) New value creation in business networks: the role of collective action in constructing system-level goals. Ind Mark Manag 67:122–133
37. Yang JB, Peng SC, (2008) Development of a customer satisfaction evaluation model for construction project management. Build Environ 43(4):458–468
38. Seidl D, Becker KH (2006) Organizations as distinction generating and processing systems: Niklas Luhmann's Contribution to Organization studies. Organization 13(1):9–35
39. Woodside AG (2014) Embrace•perform•model: complexity theory, contrarian case analysis, and multiple realities. J Bus Res 67(12):2495–2503
40. Winter M, Szczepanek T (2008) Projects and programmes as value creation processes: a new perspective and some practical implications. Int J Proj Manag 26(1):95–103
41. Leung M, Liu AM (1998) Developing a value management model–by value-goal system approach. In: Proceeding of 14th annual conference of association of researchers in construction management (ARCOM 98), vol 2. The University of Reading Reading, pp 496–505

The Big Bang, the Universe and Project Management

Now that you are familiar with the problems associated with production management theory, the idea of phenomenological value, value co-creation and elephants, I think it's time to introduce you to a new model for project management.

This model is premised on the idea that your role as a project manager is greater than simply 'delivering projects'. The model assumes you undertake value-creating activities which have nothing to do with the traditional hard paradigm of planning and controlling time, cost and scope. But to understand the model, we need to go back to the start.

No, not to the start of the book. Back to the start of the universe.

Project Management and the Big Bang

What do the universe and a project have in common?

Well, apart from the fact that many project managers think they could be the centre of both, the universe and a project both begin in pretty much the same way. Before the universe became 'the universe', all the forces, energy and elements already existed. They were just hanging around doing their own cosmological thing. Then one day, the pressure got too much and—BANG! The universe was born.

The same is true of projects. Before projects come into being, all the people, knowledge, materials, and finances needed to complete the project already exist in other organisational networks. These networks exist independently of one another. You can think of these networks like the forces that existed before the start of the universe. Everything that is needed to undertake the project is out there, but it's just sort of floating around the place. Figure 2.1 illustrates what 'life before a project' looks like.

© The Author(s), under exclusive license to Springer Nature Switzerland AG 2021
G. Usher, *Project Management in the 21ˢᵗ Century*, Management
for Professionals, https://doi.org/10.1007/978-3-030-71543-4_2

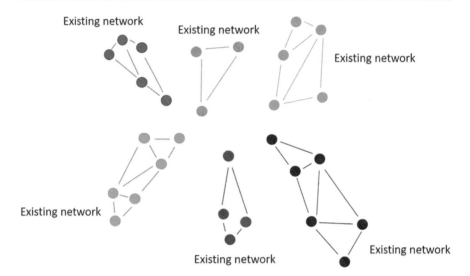

Fig. 2.1 Life before a project

Then one day, one of these existing networks discovers that it has a specific need that must be fulfilled. It also realises that it doesn't have the capability to fulfil that need. So, the network sends out a message that different capabilities are needed [1]. This message introduces a new force into the mix. This force is 'the project'. Figure 2.2 shows what the project management universe looks like, moments before a project 'big bang'.

Fig. 2.2 The need for a
project is discovered

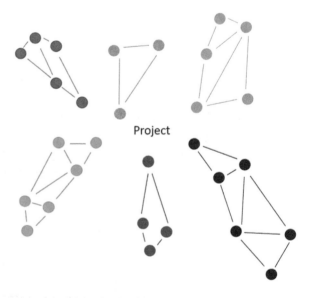

Now, rather than propel the networks apart, as the big bang did to our universe, the project creates a force of attraction. This force draws these independent networks together. Not only do they become aware of the existence of one another, but they begin to interact, for no other reason other than they are all drawn to the same project. Although these networks are now aware of the presence of each other, they have not yet begun to work on the project. However, their interactions begin to create an environment. This environment exists for the sole reason of bringing the project to life and evolving it from an idea into a reality.

The Evolution of the Project Eco-System

In biological terms, when independent networks begin interacting with one another to create a specific environment for growth, an eco-system is created. When these pre-existing networks begin to interact for the sole purpose of delivering a project, a project eco-system is created. *This eco-system is not the project*; it exists separate from the project. However, the eco-system's sole reason for 'being' is the development of the project. If there was no project, then there would be no eco-system. Conversely, the project needs the eco-system to survive. If there was no eco-system, then there would be no project. So, the eco-system and the project have an interdependent existence. One cannot exist without the other.

This interdependency means that this eco-system is specific to this project. It doesn't exist anywhere else or for any other reason other than to meet the needs of this particular project. However, each of the networks that are drawn into the eco-system also has a life outside the project eco-system. This is important because it creates a phenomenon known in systems thinking parlance as 'boundary spanning'.

The term boundary spanning comes from chaos and complexity theory. It means that the project eco-system is an 'open system' that can draw on external resources to supplement any deficiencies that exist within the project eco-system. Boundary spanning is essential in complex systems because it creates dynamic stability. Figure 2.3 shows the project eco-system and its boundary-spanning networks.

In broad terms, this is what I propose the project management 'elephant' looks like. It is both the project and the project eco-system. I'm suggesting that there is something else outside our projects that we haven't been able to see clearly because we haven't stepped far enough back in our thinking. This thing, the project eco-system, exists separate to the project, but neither the project nor the project eco-system around it can survive without the other. Together they enjoy a completely symbiotic relationship.

My new model suggests that your role as the project manager is not just to manage the project. If the project is going to become a reality, you also need to sustain the project eco-system. As we explore this model, you may find that you are already doing most of the things that need to be done. The problem is that most of what you know is based on tacit knowledge, hard-won experience and some sixth sense about what the project needs to survive and evolve. Now there is nothing wrong with that per se, it's just that it makes it very hard for you to teach anyone else how to do what you do or to explain to others why it needs to be done. So, it's really important that we understand how to create and sustain the project eco-system if we ever hope to develop a more robust understanding of our profession.

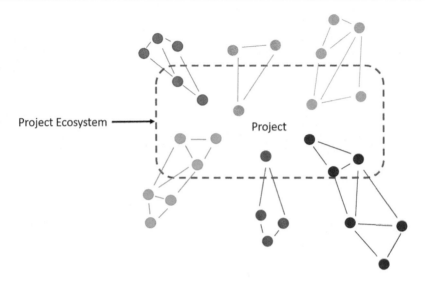

Fig. 2.3 The project eco-system and its boundary-spanning networks

Creating the Project Eco-System

Philip Drucker [2] says that most innovation is not a result of new knowledge. It is the result of seeing existing knowledge in a new way. Most innovation is simply putting things that you already know together in a way that no one has put them together before so that everyone has an 'a-ha' moment. If you have been a project manager for any length of time, I suggest that you already know most of what I am about to share with you about your project eco-system. However, I'm also hoping that I can put this together in a way that gives you some 'a-ha' moments. So, here goes…

The project eco-system is what complexity theorists call a complex adaptive system. Complex adaptive systems resist reductionist techniques because of their internal interconnectedness [3]. This interconnectedness means that a slight change at the lowest level of the network can affect the stability of the entire system, and a small shift at the highest level of the system can have large, unintended impacts on individual connections at the lowest levels.

Complex adaptive systems are never static. They constantly change as they attempt to maintain internal balance. Internal connections are constantly being broken and reformed as the system reacts to changes and attempts to capitalise on new opportunities. This constant adaption requires energy, and using energy in a bounded system has its perils. When left to their own devices, complex adaptive systems tend to do one of two things. They either lose energy and die (entropy) or they generate too much energy and fly apart (chaos).

For any complex adaptive system to survive, it needs to achieve an equilibrium between the forces that would wear it down and the forces that would tear it apart.

In other words, the system needs to find the sweet spot where it almost falls into chaos but then reorganises itself just in time to maintain stability. Complexity theorists call this sweet spot the 'edge of chaos' [4].

One of the most significant things that we have learned in recent years about complex adaptive systems is that order tends to emerge in these systems through a process of self-organisation. However, for this to happen, the system requires *order-generating rules*. These rules provide the system with the freedom it needs to operate at the edge of chaos, while at the same time limiting the extent of that chaos so overall order is maintained. Order-generating rules permit the system to concurrently generate the creative energy it needs to stave off entropy, while at the same time containing that energy so it doesn't dissipate outside the system causing it to fly apart. Order-generating rules both enable and constrain the system [5] allowing it to achieve bounded instability [6, 7].

As we discussed earlier, the project eco-system is created when pre-existing, independent networks are attracted by the force of a project. Now, it is conceivable that these independent networks could eventually reach a state of self-organisation through a process of trial and error. This process would be similar to the evolution of life on our planet. Just as primordial organisms adapted to new eco-systems by evolving into something new, it is also conceivable that the individual networks could eventually evolve together into a stable state where the project could be delivered. The only problem with adopting an evolutionary process of self-organisation is that it takes vast amounts of time and usually a lot of failed attempts to crawl out of the water. Of course, projects don't usually have a few millennia up their sleeve to let everything evolve naturally. They generally need to move a lot quicker.

One way to speed up the process of self-organisation is for an external force to impose order-generating rules on the system. For the project eco-system, this external force is you, the project manager [8, 9]. The project manager imposes order-generating rules by creating structures and mechanisms which allow the networks to dynamically organise themselves [10, 11].

But applying order-generating rules to a system is not as simple as creating a one-size-fits-all set of rules. Just as classical mechanics and quantum mechanics operate according to two very different sets of rules [12–14], so too the rules that govern complex adaptive systems operate differently depending on what level of the system the rules are applied to. These two different groups of rules can be thought of as *system rules* and *local rules* [15, 16]. For our new project management model, I'll call these eco-system level rules and project level rules.

Complex adaptive systems operate best when they have broad rules imposed on them at the eco-system level. Conversely, they operate best at the project level when they have more prescriptive rules. This dichotomy between eco-system level and project level operating rules provides both freedom and control within the same system. The broad rules at the eco-system level allow the existing networks to interface with the world outside the eco-system, while the project level rules provide the existing networks with a firm grasp on the 'rules of the game' inside the eco-system.

The need to have different operating rules for both system and project levels can create paradoxical challenges. You need to allow the eco-system enough freedom to boundary span and interface with the wider environment with as little constraint as possible. At the same time, you need to maintain enough control within the eco-system to create structure and order. Achieving this balance requires a special blend of skills. It requires a person who has both technical and organisational skills. A person who understands how to develop and operationalise strategy. A person who can act as visionary, guide, facilitator and umpire simultaneously [17]. But most of all, this person also needs to have a detailed understanding of how to sustain the project eco-system.

So, let me ask you this, 'Do you have a detailed understanding of how to sustain the project eco-system?'

At first, I thought I didn't, but the more I thought about it, the more I realise I probably know a lot more than I gave myself credit for, and you know what? I bet you know a lot more about it than you think as well. In fact, I suspect that if you are a half-decent project manager, you already know about these rules—you just don't know you know.

At both the eco-system level and the project level, there are four categories of order-generating rules. These rules govern *provisioning* [18], *regulating* [19, 20], *supporting* [21] and *culturalising* [9].

If you fail to put any one of these rule groups in place, both your eco-system and your project will struggle. Of course, establishing these rules doesn't completely remove the potential for catastrophic failure, but having them in place does help the networks in your eco-system to self-organise.

Let's have a look at the order-generating rules one at a time.

Eco-System Level Provisioning Rules

The first category of eco-system level, order-generating rules are the *provisioning* rules. The function of this group of rules is to ensure that provisions are available to the eco-system when they are needed. In a natural eco-system, like a rainforest or savannah, the eco-system requires three types of provisions—food, water and raw materials [24]. In a project eco-system, these provisions can be thought of as time (food), finances (water) and knowledge (raw material).

Time

When project managers think about 'time', our focus is usually on how little we have available to complete our project. Beginning a project with a 'scarcity' mindset can impair our judgement and cause us to make mistakes that can ultimately decide the success or failure of our project.

For example, a scarcity mindset can cause us to rush into getting started. From the moment we engage with the project, we feel time poor. This creates an insidious illusion, where we mistakenly feel that we have no time to spare. This scarcity mindset can have devastating effects at the eco-system level, not the least of which is that it makes time our enemy.

When we make time our enemy, we instinctively want to control it. We resort to our 'factory default setting' and think that the most important thing we can do with time is to plan it, monitor it and measure it. We try to control time by putting together minutely detailed schedules that confirm that we can reach the required project outcome before our time runs out. We document every step, assign a duration to it, and then map out the 'correct' sequence for achieving our time goal.

Now, don't get me wrong. I am a big fan of planning stuff out. You should see the roadmap on my wall for this book! But this level of detailed planning is not an eco-system level *provisioning* rule. It's a project-level rule. At the eco-system level, our role is not to *control* time but to *make* time.

'Oh sure', I can hear you think, 'I'll just pop over to the time factory and make myself some more time. While I'm at it, I'll add another 3 hours to my day, so that I can get home and see the kids before they go to bed'.

First of all, no one likes a cynic.

Secondly, what you are failing to grasp is that, philosophically, time is an abstract concept. It doesn't actually exist. It only exists because we choose to believe it exists. The simple truth is we all 'make time' every day. Every day we make time to do the things that are important to us. Understanding this is critical to the survival of your eco-system, and here's why.

Every complex adaptive system requires time to develop, evolve and create internal stability. This is particularly true when these systems are human systems with complex social bonds. Our eco-system is one of these systems. It requires strong social connections to remain stable.

The networks that operate in our eco-system need time to bond. They need time to understand how they will work together. They need time to learn how they all like to operate. These networks need time to learn to trust one another and to create their own culture.

I think we can all agree that having this time available to bond the new team together is a great idea. However, what usually happens is that by the time sponsoring network calls in the project team, they have often 'used up' a lot of time and now have an overwhelming sense of urgency to get the project started.

I understand this desire to jump in and get started, I really do. This 'Here, hold my beer!' attitude is one of the reasons why I love working with project managers. We are people of action. But regardless of how appealing the 'jump first, look later' approach is in appeasing the emotional needs of the sponsoring network, it brings with it some potential long-term problems. That's why it's vital that you make time for the networks to bond, regardless of how much pressure there is to get the project started.

Deciding to slow down and create time, is often overlooked by inexperienced project managers who confuse the urgent for the important. Getting the project started might seem urgent, but, as we are learning, our role is not just to deliver the project; it is also about managing the project eco-system—and making time for your eco-system to develop is important. If you fail to 'make time' at the start, you increase the risk of system instability. While this may not end up with the system completely flying apart, it will almost certainly result in connection failures between the networks which cause delays, misunderstandings and abortive works and will ultimately reduce the effectiveness and efficiency of your project team.

To provision your eco-system for success, you need to make time for the networks to forge the relationships they will need to survive the project journey. You need to give them an opportunity to understand how they will add value and how that value can be co-created with the other network members, and most of all give them time to build trust and create their own unique culture.

Finance

This element of the project eco-system's provisioning is perhaps best explained by Rod Tidwell in the movie, Jerry Maguire—'Show me the money!'

Newsflash! Finances are needed to sustain your project. Finances are the water supply of your eco-system. If the finances stop flowing, all the networks in your eco-system will either die or move off to find a new supply. However, at the system level, your concern isn't the management of finances (i.e. controlling costs); your concern is the supply of finances.

One of the first things you need to do before engaging with your project is to check your finance supply. Before starting anything else, you need to confirm, for yourself, that there are enough finances available to undertake the project.

Just in case you weren't paying attention, I'll write that again:

Before starting anything else, you need to confirm, **for yourself,** *that there are enough finances available to undertake the project.*

Whatever you do, don't assume that just because a sponsor has decided to undertake a project, that someone up in the C-Suite has approved enough finances to complete the job. Sponsors are notoriously bad at underestimating how much money they need to put aside for a project to be completed. So, YOU must be the one who confirms this. This means interrogating business cases, fighting to have contingencies included, and doing everything you can to make the sponsoring network understand that a figure on a spreadsheet does not represent the complexities of the journey on which you are all about to embark.

If you determine that the sponsoring network does not have adequate finances to complete the project, then it is incumbent on you to clearly state 'we need to find more money or we need to stop'. The project manager is the one person in this whole process that cannot afford to just play nice and just 'go with the flow'.

No project manager on earth can cost control their way out of an initial finance deficit. It's that simple, you're not a wizard. You can't magic your way out of an initial budget hole. If you start a project without adequate financing, there are only two possible outcomes; you will either end up having to reduce scope mid-project, or you will have to reduce the quality of the final product. Neither of these options provides a particularly rewarding value experience. So, don't be foolish enough to fall into a deficit trap at the start of a project.

But why should this be your job?

Because once you commence the project, no one will remember there was a finance deficit at the start. They will just start blaming you for not controlling the costs at a project level.

So, unless you have a masochistic streak and enjoy regular flagellation, I strongly recommend that you address the finance supply issue *before* setting out on your project journey.

Ok, let's assume that you have confirmed that the sponsoring network has set aside enough finances to complete the project. That's a great start, but it's not the full extent of this specific *provisioning* rule. At the eco-system level, you also need to consider your distribution system.

Once you have confirmed that there is a large enough supply, you need to ensure that the finances keep flowing into, and through, your eco-system. Like the water in a natural eco-system, the supply needs to make its way from the storage facility (i.e. a dam) to the end-users. To do this, you need to keep the trunk lines of your eco-system clear of potential blockages so that the finances can flow freely. You do this by establishing clear mechanisms and systems for payment (usually through the vehicle of a contract). You ensure there is alignment between prime and sub-contracts, and you make sure the sponsor is aware, well in advance, when new injections of finances will be required. This distribution of finances is vitally important; the last thing your delicate eco-system needs is a drought.

Knowledge

For a project to evolve from an idea into reality, it needs the right raw materials. At the eco-system level, these raw materials are not commodities like steel, concrete, electronics or cabling. Those are project-level provisions. The eco-system level raw materials are far more important and far more difficult to find. The raw materials needed at this level are the right ideas and knowledge.

If you step far enough away from any project, you will see that all projects are really the same thing. A problem that needs to be solved. Projects are one of the vehicles that people use to move from one state of existence (i.e. where we have a problem) to another state of existence (i.e. where the problem is solved) [25]. Everything after that is just details.

Adopting this higher perspective helps us understand the provisioning we need to do at the eco-system level. At this level, our aim is to ensure that the eco-system can solve the specific project 'problem' and all its associated challenges. Thus, provisioning at the eco-system level simply becomes a function of having access to the right knowledge at the right time.

It has been argued that one of the least understood functions of the project manager is the role of gatekeeper [26]. A gatekeeper is the person who decides who can and who can't be part of the eco-system. Project managers do this in many ways. We assist the sponsor in deciding what technical disciplines they need to solve their problem, thereby excluding other technical disciplines. We draft up tender documents that create barriers and hurdles to entry into the project eco-system. We evaluate tenders and give recommendations and advice on who should be selected to enter the project eco-system and therefore, by definition, exclude others.

Not only do we decide who gets to enter the system, but we also make decisions about who gets to stay in the eco-system. We punish underperformance through contract administration and advocate for the removal of poor-performing networks from the eco-system. As project managers, we have a great deal of influence over who gets to stay within the boundaries of our little world. Whether we realise it or not, no one gets into the project eco-system unless we let them in, and no one stays in the project eco-system after we have decided they should leave. It is a function of our role that has both great authority and great responsibility.

Having this authority allows us to control our eco-system by deciding who is in and who is out. By default, this means we have the authority to decide what knowledge is available both within, and too, the networks inside our eco-system. This authority creates a responsibility. Because we are the gatekeeper, it is our responsibility to ensure the eco-system is adequately provisioned with the right knowledge at the right time, so that the project problem and its associated challenges can be overcome.

Summary

So, lets recap. At the eco-system level, the project manager creates order-generating rules that *provision* the eco-system to deliver the project. The basic provisions required are time, finance and knowledge. The specific rules for each of these are summarised in Table 2.1.

Eco-System Level Regulating Rules

We've already looked at the problems that complex adaptive systems have with energy. They either run out and collapse or they have too much and explode. Depending on the system, they may need to draw energy in, expel energy out and, in some cases, fluctuate between both at different times just to survive.

Table 2.1 Eco-system level provisioning rules

Provisioning	Requirement	Eco-system level rule
	Time	Make time for your eco-system to develop internal stability
	Finance	Confirm there is an adequate supply, and make sure it keeps flowing
	Knowledge	Ensure the right knowledge is available within the eco-system

To understand how regulating rules work at the eco-system level, we need to draw on some concepts from the field of physics, specifically thermodynamics. There are many laws that govern the field of thermodynamics, and some of them you may already know. However, the one that is of the most interest for our eco-system level regulating rules is the law of conservation of energy. This law states that energy cannot be created nor destroyed, but it can be transferred or transformed. Regulating the energy in our eco-system requires us to either transfer or transform energy regularly.

Balancing the energy of your project eco-system is essential. You need enough energy to fuel creative innovation and problem-solving, but not so much that passion overcomes reason. One of the best ways to regulate the energy of your eco-system is through the judicious use of conflict.

Conflict is essential to the development of all human activities. It has been described as the driving force behind all growth [24]. Whenever there is a limited supply of resources, conflict is inevitable. Whenever passionate ideas, ideals or people are thrown together, conflict is inevitable. As Campbell [25] notes, '…Conflict is a natural and inevitable part of every relationship…'. The relationships that exist in your eco-system are no exception. Conflict is important for us because *conflict generates energy*.

So often we approach the idea of conflict with feelings of negativity because we associate conflict with ideas of violence and destruction. However, conflict can be viewed in other ways as well. There is a school of thought that suggests conflict is amoral. It is neither good nor bad. It can be a vehicle for growth or regression. This school of thought suggests that it is not the conflict itself that is important, rather it is our management of that conflict which determines whether the conflict is a constructive or destructive force [26].

Your ability to regulate the energy in your eco-system will be in direct correlation to your ability to manage conflict. You need to know how to transfer or transform energy into or out of your eco-system, by either creating or defusing conflict.

Transfer Energy In

There are times when your eco-system will need an energy injection. Do you know the signs that indicate an energy injection is required? Do you know how to inject that energy?

One of the first indicators that your eco-system is devolving is a lack of heat and friction. We often think that a lack of conflict is a good sign, when in fact it could be a sign that the system is getting ready to collapse in on itself. As project managers, our goal is not to create a conflict-free zone but to create an eco-system where peace is achieved '…not [through] the absence of conflict but [through] the presence of creative alternatives for responding to conflict – alternatives to passive or aggressive responses, alternatives to violence' [27].

Conflict can be a powerful creative force. If conflict already exists in your eco-system, you must harness the energy generated by that conflict. If conflict doesn't already exist, you might need to create some.

Wait, what? Why would I want to create conflict in my eco-system?

Great question! In fact, there are several reasons why you might want to create conflict in your project eco-system.

First, conflict creates adaptability. When people discuss issues that they are passionate about, there is the potential for conflict. When team members are forced to scramble for the same limited resources, there is the potential for conflict. When people are forced to work together to overcome challenges, there is a potential for conflict. These conflicts can only be managed in one of two ways—through violence or through adaptation. Our goal is the latter. As the networks in your eco-system move closer together, they will undoubtedly have friction points that create conflict. Every one of these is an opportunity to adapt to new ways of doing things. However, it's important to understand that it is not always your job to resolve these conflicts. It is important that the networks in your eco-system self-organise and find ways to resolve these conflicts themselves. This will teach them to be both adaptable and resilient, qualities that your eco-system must develop if it is to survive the unexpected challenges that the project will create.

Second, conflicts generate new ideas. As Mayer [24] highlights, '…conflict provides a wonderfully rich field for challenging people to think differently about the problems they face…' (p. 81). One of the dangers faced by a project eco-system without conflict is the development of 'groupthink'. Groupthink results from a desire for harmony and conformity. It is a form of conflict avoidance that ultimately results in irrational and dysfunctional decision-making. The desire to 'not rock the boat' stifles disagreement and debate and almost certainly ensures the knowledge that you have provisioned into your eco-system becomes ineffective. You need to challenge and break down this conflict-avoiding behaviour because some of the best ideas arise out of the greatest conflicts. Conflicts create an energy source that drives action, demands creative problem-solving and inspires innovation.

Finally, conflicts increase the probability of achieving your project goals. When the networks in your eco-system are forced into conflict, and then work together to achieve a mutually beneficial outcome, they learn to work with one another for the common good. Having these individual networks learn to forego their individual goals and find mutually beneficial outcomes is fundamental to the maturation of your eco-system and ultimately for the successful completion of the project. As each of these networks navigates through conflict, they grow individually and bond collectively. Every conflict they work through strengthens them as a project-focused network and increases their potential to overcome challenges.

There are many ways that we can transfer energy into our eco-system. We can do it by pairing up individuals who are passionate, but who might have different views on what or how something should be accomplished. We can do it by challenging assumptions about the purpose of the project, some attribute of the business case or the reasons behind certain decisions. We can do it by making networks compete for the same resources (like time or money) or by forcing designers or contractors, stakeholders or sponsors to achieve a goal in a different way to what they normally would. In other words, you transfer energy into your eco-system by shaking it up and using whatever means you have available.

Understanding that conflict can generate creative energy in your eco-system leads us to the first regulating order-generating rule—*create constructive conflict to stave off entropy.*

Transfer Energy Out

Now, let's not be naïve. Not all conflicts result in positive or creative energy. There will be conflicts that create enough negative energy to push your eco-system to the brink of destruction. Ignoring these conflicts is to court disaster. So, whether we like it or not, we have to regulate this energy as well, and the only way to do that is to get neck-deep in the middle of these destructive conflicts.

Within the project eco-system, there are seven areas that can give rise to conflicts [28]; these are:

1. Project priorities.
2. Administrative procedures.
3. Technical opinions.
4. Resourcing constraints.
5. Cost estimates.
6. Scheduling and sequencing.
7. Personality conflicts.

Research by Thamhain and Wilemon [29] indicates that the *intensity* of the conflicts generated from the first six of these areas will vary throughout the project life-cycle. However, the *likelihood* of personality-based conflicts remains constant from project inception to project completion, making them some of the most difficult conflicts you will ever have to manage.

While personality conflicts may not always appear to have the intensity of the conflicts that arise from the other six areas, they have the potential to be far more destructive. It has been my experience that conflicts which arise from any of the first six areas can lead to positive outcomes. But unresolved, personality-based conflicts almost always go very bad, very quickly.

Because personality conflicts may not appear to be as 'explosive' as conflicts over things like scheduling, cost or technical opinions, it is easy to miss the energy that a slow-burn, simmering personality conflict can generate. What's more, we often prefer to deal with the explosive, non-personal conflicts, because these issues are more likely to resolve using a logical and rational approach [25].

Choosing to avoid personality-based conflicts within your eco-system may appear to be the easiest path. However, as Mayer [24] highlights '…when we avoid one conflict, we may be setting up another…when we choose to engage in one conflict, we are likely avoiding another…' (p. 96). In other words, choosing to ignore a simmering personality-based conflict in your eco-system will only result in having to deal with different conflicts later.

I have found that choosing to 'stay out' of personality-based conflicts within my eco-system never fixes anything. It just creates a myriad of other conflicts that I have to deal with. As the two opponents continue to seethe internally, they will become covertly antagonistic towards one another. They will oppose each other's ideas, not on merit, but on principle. They will interact calmly at the project meeting and then coordinate passive/aggressive attacks on each other once they leave the room. They will white-ant good ideas, put up irrational roadblocks and in some cases flatly refuse to allow a project to proceed passed a specific milestone for no other reason other than pay-back against the other person. Trust me when I tell you ignoring personality-based conflicts is a sure-fire path to the destruction of your project eco-system.

So, how do we go about transferring this energy out of the eco-system so that it doesn't end up going ballistic. Well, unfortunately, there is no algorithm or checklist that I can give you. Each personality-based conflict is as different as the people involved. However, not having a checklist is not the same thing as not having a strategy, and here's mine.

First and foremost, you need to develop negotiating skills *before* the eco-system is created. The moment your project eco-system begins to form, you will have different people beginning to fight for resources, express personal opinions and have differing views on what could and should be done. It's no good waiting until you are in the middle of that to start learning the skills. Get ahead of the game—enrol in some formal training, read whatever you can get your hands on and take every opportunity to practice the craft. Often our desire to 'not get involved' is not for the self-righteous reasons we tell ourselves, it's because we are afraid that we don't have the necessary skills to successfully or constructively resolve the issues. This simply isn't good enough. We need to assume that conflict within the project eco-system is inevitable and prepare ourselves accordingly. *Si vis Pacem, Para Bellum*: if you desire peace, prepare for war.

Next, engage in the conflict with the primary focus of ensuring that relationships remain intact. Remember you are creating an outlet for the destructive energy to leave your eco-system, not proclaiming yourself to be judge, jury and executioner. Your eco-system is only sustainable while the relational bonds between individual members remain unbroken. So, protecting them must be your primary focus.

Finally, you need to understand that personality-based conflicts within your eco-system are inevitable. There is no use sticking your head in the sand and hoping they either won't occur or they will resolve themselves. That's not a strategy, it's an abdication of responsibilities. I believe one of the best strategies for regulating energy in your eco-system is modelling a conflict-positive culture.

A conflict-positive culture encourages the networks in your eco-system to be OK with conflict. You can regulate the energy in your project eco-system by explaining early and regularly that you not only anticipate conflict, but you encourage it. By getting ahead of the game, you get to be the one who sets the rules of engagement. You want everyone involved to feel they can tackle issues openly and head-on. That way you can dissipate negative energy while it is only at low levels of intensity, rather than waiting until it becomes a Chernobyl-style event.

Understanding that negative conflict is both inevitable and potentially cataclysmic for your eco-system leads us to the second regulating order-generating rule— *identify and release destructive energy quickly to defuse explosions.*

Transforming Energy

The third and final eco-system regulating rule has to do with the transformation of energy. As we have seen, there will be times when you will need to both introduce additional energy into and release excess energy from your eco-system. The ability to transfer energy into and out of the system is fundamental for a complex adaptive system.

However, what about the energy that is generated within the system and needs to stay in the system for it to operate? Do you need to manage this as well? Yep, you sure do!

Ensuring that we have sufficient energy conserved in our eco-system is vital. It ensures the system has the capacity to undertake the required project work. However, the energy generated within the system is not always in the form that we need it. Sometimes we need to transform that energy so it becomes useful.

There are many types of energy stored or being generated in your eco-system. There's potential energy stored within the ideas and knowledge. There is energy stored within the network resources that have gathered around the project. There is the energy generated through conflicts within your eco-system. All these energy sources need to be transformed so they can ultimately be utilised by your project.

In the last section, we looked at the importance of creating a conflict-positive attitude to release excess negative energy from the eco-system. But, energy transformation requires a different strategy. Converting energy from one form to another in your eco-system requires a positive-conflict attitude.

A positive-conflict attitude encourages people to engage in conflict in a manner that creates positive outcomes. Whether that comes from sharing novel ideas, challenging assumptions, having robust discussions and even engaging in fiery debate. As a project manager, you want this type of energy being generated. As we have repeatedly discussed, conflict is not a problem; it's a necessity. It's only when the conflict generates negative outcomes that we have a problem.

Creating a positive-conflict attitude in the eco-system is a matter of setting some ground rules so you can manage the energy conversion process. This is not as difficult as it sounds, because we already know where most of the conflict will be generated. It will come from friction at one of the seven areas identified by Hill [28]. So, if we know where the conflict will be generated, we can manage the energy conversion process by getting ahead of the game before the fun starts. As Sun-Tzu says 'Victorious warriors win first and then go to war, while defeated warriors go to war first and then seek to win' [30].

One strategy for creating a positive-conflict attitude in the project eco-system is to make the first six of these conflict areas (excluding personality conflicts) standing agenda items at meetings and encouraging open discussion and debate. By leading everyone into the areas of greatest contention, and managing any conflict that arises, you can transform the heat of friction into better outcomes for the group. Or, to put this another way, you can convert conflict into progress.

Another way to manage the energy conversion process is to make sure that when conflict does arise, you work the problem, not the symptoms. All too often, we focus our attention on trying to alleviate the effect of conflicts without understanding the reason we have a conflict in the first place. This is especially true when the conflict is heated. Most people have a desire to live our lives in peace and harmony, and project managers are no exception. When conflict begins to generate heat within our eco-system, we often try to return to a state of peace and harmony as quickly as possible by alleviating the symptoms. While this might have the immediate effect of making everyone feel better, all it does is push the problems further down the track and lets the energy build to the point where an explosive outcome is a real possibility. Our eco-system will be much healthier if we take the time to find the root cause of the conflict at the time it occurs. But how can we do this? It's simple. Just act like a child.

My granddaughter is a master at getting to the root cause of everything, and she does with one word—'Why?' But just asking it once is never enough for her. She just keeps asking the same question until she has drilled right down to the bedrock of an issue.

Granddaughter:	*"Can I have a puppy at your place?"*
Me:	*"No, darling"*
Granddaughter:	*"Why?"*
Me:	*"I just don't think it's a good idea".*
Granddaughter:	*"Why?"*
Me:	*"Because we don't have enough space"*
Granddaughter:	*"Why?"*
Me:	*"Because puppies need a lot of room, and we don't have enough room in the backyard for a puppy".*
Granddaughter:	*"Oh, ok. Can you get a bigger backyard?"*
Me:	*"No, darling"*
Granddaughter:	*"Why?"*

... and on and on and on it goes. You get the picture.

When our eco-system is infused with a positive-conflict attitude we are not afraid of conflict, so we are not afraid to keep digging into that conflict until we hit the bedrock of the issues. Once we reach that point, we can then start the process of transforming the energy of conflict into progress by resolving the actual issues rather than just alleviating the symptoms.

Understanding that eco-systems need a certain amount of energy to survive, and that energy is generated through conflict, leads us to the final regulating order-generating rule—*convert conflict into progress*.

Summary

Let's recap. We now know that, at the eco-system level, the regulation rules are about energy, whether that's energy which needs to be transferred into, or out of the eco-system, or energy that needs to be transformed within the eco-system.

The specific rules for each of these are summarised in Table 2.2.

Table 2.2 Eco-system level regulating rules

Regulating	Requirement	Eco-system level rule
	Transfer energy in	Create constructive conflict to stave off entropy
	Transfer energy out	Identify and release destructive energy quickly to defuse explosions
	Transforming energy	Convert conflict into progress

Eco-System Level Supporting Rules

The third group of eco-system level rules are the *supporting* rules. These rules are focussed on clearing obstacles which might impede the healthy development of your eco-system. As we have seen, the eco-system provisioning rules provide the necessary resources, and the eco-system regulating rules control the energy in the system. But neither of these guarantees that your eco-system will develop the way you want it too.

If there are obstacles which prevent the natural development of your eco-system, you may find that the entire eco-system becomes deformed as the networks attempt to self-organise around these obstacles. These ad hoc workarounds can impact the efficiency and structural integrity of the entire eco-system. To overcome this, you need to implement eco-system *supporting* rules that create political stability and knowledge bridging.

Political Stability

Not all the challenges that your eco-system will face will come from inside the system itself. Sometimes your eco-system will face challenges from external sources as well. These external challenges can create big problems because your eco-system needs a stable, external environment if it is going to have any chance of surviving.

At the early stages of your eco-system's life, when the networks are beginning to understand how they will interact with one another, it is extremely vulnerable to external political instability. If your boundary-spanning networks sense there is any lack of support for the project, or any danger that the project might not proceed, they will hold off on developing social and economic interactions with the other networks. They do this as a means of self-preservation, but this failure to create these interactions can stunt the growth of your eco-system and, in the worst cases, cause some of the networks to withdraw from your eco-system altogether.

But the good news is that you can create external stability for your eco-system by interrogating and understanding 'why' the project exists. In other words, we must understand the strategic drivers that created the need for the project in the first place.

Understanding these strategic drivers can be the most important information that you will ever possess. If you know why the sponsor needs to undertake the project, you can use this information to create the political stability your eco-system needs.

Once I was working as a consultant project manager for a service-based organisation which wanted to embark on a large development project. This organisation has some very smart people at the helm, but they had never undertaken a large property development project before. Acknowledging that they had a lack of skill in this area, the board hired my firm to develop the initial feasibility study and business case.

My very first action as the project manager frustrated the crap out of them. Instead of jumping in and getting started with the business case, I insisted on meeting with their senior executive team, one by one, and talking with each of them about why this project was important (see *Provisioning—Time*). The sponsor's rep was annoyed that I didn't start by doing 'real' project management work—you know like creating a scoping document or putting together the cost plans. Luckily I was able to convince him to give me enough rope so he could hang me later if he wanted to.

These first few weeks were invaluable. They gave me both a strong understanding of the ethos of the organisation I was working with, and it helped me understand the strategic drivers behind why the project was necessary. More importantly, I was able to work out who, at the executive level of the organisation, was a supporter or a detractor of the project. I also found out which executives were non-plussed about the whole development.

Fast forward 6 months to the completion of the business case, my feasibility study showed the development was going to cost a lot more than the sponsors had first thought (see *Provisioning—Finance*). In fact, it was so much more that it created a significant schism in the sponsor's executive team. Some wanted to abandon the project immediately, others wanted to continue. In other words, I encountered some significant external, political instability.

However, because I had made time to understand 'why' the organisation wanted to undertake the development, I was able to talk to their executive team about more than just the hard numbers in the business case. We were able to discuss the strategic impact to the organisation if they didn't go ahead with the project. After several meetings and a lot of discussions, we finally came up with a solution that fulfilled the strategic goals of the organisation and was unanimously supported by the executive team and, perhaps more importantly, one for which they were willing to release additional funding.

This is what I mean by creating external political stability. If I had simply started the business case, the project would have died at that board meeting because I would have gone to that meeting knowing *what* the board wanted done, but not *why* they wanted it done. The only way my eco-system was able to survive was because I was able to create political stability in the external environment.

As it turned out, I needed to repeatedly draw on this stability as the project evolved. As with any project, I encountered new and unforeseen challenges. Most of these frightened the executive team who had never undertaken a large project before; but because we had all agreed *why* the project was required, we were able to return time and time to that understanding and reiterate that the *why* was more important than just money or time. Because I had established this political stability and had regularly returned to reinforce it, I was able to shield the networks in my eco-system from many of the issues that might have caused them to become fearful and move into a self-preservation mode.

Knowledge Bridging

The networks which inhabit your eco-system normally 'live' somewhere else. I like to think of them as tribes who live in different regions but who have been drawn to a common watering hole.

Each of these tribes has their own way of life. They have their own cultures, customs and languages. These languages have developed to express complex and highly detailed information as efficiently as possible and are a great way of sharing knowledge…provided you speak the language.

Now don't get confused, I'm not talking about whether everyone in the project team can speak English or Cantonese or Farsi. I'm talking about the *other* languages that your networks speak. Languages that are made up of jargon, acronyms and industry buzzwords.

How do you spot one of these other languages? Well, tell me if this seems familiar.

You've just had a detailed conversation with the [*insert tribe member here*] who spent the last 20 min explaining a particular challenge or problem that they are facing in the project. At around the 5 min mark, your eyes started to glaze over and your brain switched to static and the only thought you had was 'Huh?'

If you've ever experienced that, then you know what I mean by the other languages.

The problem in this scenario is that a great deal of detailed information has been transmitted, but you leave the discussion having no idea what was actually said. The knowledge this tribe member brings to your eco-system is worthless because you don't speak their language. These types of communication misfires are happening every day in your eco-system, and every time it happens, 'knowledge gaps' are created between the networks.

The second eco-system supporting rule is aimed at overcoming these knowledge gaps. To span these divides and ensure knowledge is effectively transferred within the eco-system, you need to build *knowledge bridges*.

These bridges need to be built in two directions, horizontally and vertically. A horizontal knowledge bridge spans the disconnect between networks within the eco-system, while a vertical knowledge bridge spans the disconnect between the individuals within the eco-system and the network decision-makers that live outside the eco-system [31].

Whether you are building a horizontal or vertical bridge, you always use the same process. Textbooks call this process decontextualisation and recontextualisation [32]. The decontextualisation/recontextualisation process simply means gathering knowledge from one network using their language, distilling this down to key messages and salient points and then presenting those key messages and salient points to another network in their language. Basically, you become an interpreter.

I think most of you reading this book will understand the principle of the horizontal knowledge bridges, but perhaps you are struggling with how a vertical bridge works.

One example, from my experience, of creating a vertical knowledge bridge, was when a 'good idea fairy' visited a sponsor following a site inspection and he decided he wanted to change the floor plate of a building that was already under construction.

I nodded and wrote this down to show that I was taking him seriously, and then at the next project governance board (PGB) meeting, I tabled the request, explained the basics of weight transference in a structure, the problems of services coordination and the building approval processes. After that, I gave the PGB the key messages in a language they could understand, 'This change will cost you an extra $5 million and delay the project by 6-9 months'. Once I had interpreted the key points into a language they could understand it turned out that the change in the floorplate wasn't that important after all. The end result? One good idea fairy dead and one vertical knowledge bridge successfully built.

Summary

OK, so let's recap. At the eco-system level, the supporting rules are focussed on clearing obstacles which might impede the healthy development of your eco-system. Specifically, these include creating external political stability and building knowledge bridges. The eco-system supporting rules are summarised in Table 2.3.

Table 2.3 Eco-system level supporting rules

Supporting	Requirement	Eco-system level rule
	Political stability	Protect the project eco-system from external political instability
	Knowledge bridging	Interpret key messages and salient points into languages the different networks can understand

Eco-System Level Culturalising Rules

The fourth and last group of eco-system level rules are the *culturalising* rules. These rules help establish the social connections necessary for value co-creation to occur. These rules fuse individual networks into a cohesive unit inside your eco-system so that the entire system is stable, adaptive and focussed.

There are only two eco-system level *culturalising* rules. They answer two fundamental questions: 'Who are we?' and 'Why are we here?'

Shared Identity

The people who join your eco-system already have a range of identities which they have developed over time. They have their personal identity which helps them decide who they are in the world and how they want to behave, and they have the collective identity of the networks which existed before your project was even a thing.

Our personal identities are comprised of the qualities, beliefs, ethics, morals, looks and expressions of self. These identities help us decide who we are in the world. Our personal identities define how we perceive ourselves and are the single largest contributor to our understanding of our world.

Our personal identity taints our view of the world. It is our personal identity that helps us work out if the world is a positive or negative place for us to live in. It goes to the basic questions of survival. Should I risk building trust with this person or should be building defences? Ultimately our personal identity drives how we express our true self in any given social situation.

Layered on top of our personal identities are the collective identities of the groups that we choose to become part of. The collective identity of any group is the deciding factor in whether a person will join that group. If a person feels their personal identity aligns with the collective identity of the group, they will join it, remain part of it and work to strengthen and reinforce that collective identity. If their personal identity doesn't align with the collective identity, they will either leave or, perhaps worse, stay and create negative and toxic social interactions within the network. As project managers, we need to be aware that the networks which created our eco-system already have their own, very strong collective identities, and these identities can have huge impacts on the effectiveness of our eco-system.

I firmly believe that developing a positive collective identity for your eco-system is the defining factor on whether your project will ultimately create value. Creating a shared identity takes time, and it needs to be carefully guided and crafted. Unless you take deliberate actions to build the shared identity of your eco-system, the identity that develops could end up being something destructive rather than constructive. Trust me when I tell you enduring the project journey with a team that has developed a destructive, hostile or defensive identity will be the hardest project of your life.

But the most important message here is that, as the project manager, you get to decide, and then develop, the shared identity of the eco-system. You do this through the use of rituals and beliefs, as well as modelled and explicit values. These can be completely unrelated to the actual delivery of the project, but they will significantly impact that delivery. Scheduling social gatherings, reinforcing preferred behaviours and sending out positive messages like overcoming challenges or making progress, as well as basic stuff like 'walking the talk', all build the culture and traditions of your eco-system. These actions become the foundation of your eco-system's shared identity and will motivate those inside your eco-system towards mutually beneficial outcomes [33, 34].

Shared Vision

Initially, the existing networks were attracted to the project because they felt there was something in it for them. Their desire to be involved was driven by individual gain. However, your project eco-system needs a higher purpose than each individual network just asking, 'What's in this for me?'

That self-centred thinking will eventually create problems for everyone, especially when the desires of different networks conflict with another. To create an eco-system that can support the evolution of your project, there must be mutual benefits for all the networks involved.

Wasko and Faraj [35] have argued that extracting mutual beneficial outcomes from a complex adaptive system requires a specific agent to create shared value and goals. Can you guess who that specific agent is? Yep, you!

For the networks who have joined your eco-system, the shared goal is an easy one to define: The shared goal is the project. However, the development of shared values can be more difficult to develop because, as I mentioned earlier, value is subjective.

To build a shared vision, you need to make some deliberate choices about the eco-system's purpose and identity. You need to get the networks in your eco-system to look beyond their initial, self-serving reason for getting involved, by creating a vision that leaves a positive legacy on people and communities [36]. But how can you do this? Well, perhaps this parable will help.

Once upon a time, there was a king who decided that he wanted to build the most magnificent Cathedral in the land. He summoned three renowned stonemasons and told them his dream. He gave each of the stonemasons' responsibility for one section of the Cathedral. The king then assigned each of them ten workers to assist them with their task.

Some weeks went by and the King decided that he wanted to see the progress of his project. When he approached the Cathedral he noticed something very strange. The first section of the Cathedral had a wall, but it was only a quarter completed. The next section had a wall, but it was only half completed. The third and final section, not only had a completed wall but the workmanship and detailing were extraordinary.

The King went over to the first section and asked the workers, "What are you doing?" Together they replied, "Exactly what the stonemason told us to do, sire". So, the King asked, 'What did the stonemason tell you to do?". Together they replied, "Lay some stones sire".

The King then moved on to the second section and asked the workers, "What are you doing?" Together they replied, "Exactly what the stonemason told us to do, sire". So, the King asked, 'What did the stonemason tell you to do?". Together they replied, "Build a wall, sire".

Finally, the king moved on to the third section. He marvelled at the precision and level of detail that had been included in the new construction. He asked the workers, "What are you doing?" Together they replied, "Exactly what the stonemason told us to do, sire". So, the King asked, 'What did the stonemason tell you to do?". Together they replied, "Build a Cathedral fit for a king, sire".

Can you work out why the last stonemason got a better outcome from her team? It's simple once you understand the secret.

People need to feel that their work matters.

In our parable, there is no real technical difference between laying stones and building a cathedral. The activities required for both are the same, but the difference could not be greater. The difference has to do with the concept of value co-creation. For the workers, the difference was how they felt about what they were doing. One group was laying stones, and the other group was constructing a monument that will span the ages. There was no difference in the work required, just in the mindset.

Every single one of us has a 'hard-wired' desire to do something that matters with our lives. This need can be satisfied by accomplishing things that we believe have value. As a project manager, you can access this hard-wired desire and create fulfilling work for everyone in your eco-system by establishing a system of value co-creation.

Building a shared vision in your eco-system is more than just explaining what needs to be done. It's more than ensuring the project outcomes are aligned with the strategic goals of the sponsoring network. You need to be the third stonemason. You must create a vision that's bigger than just 'delivering the project'. Creating a shared vision of meaning and purpose is fundamental to your eco-system's value co-creation process. Done well, a shared vision creates something that surpasses just the cost of the project. It creates value for everyone.

Summary

So, lets recap. As a project manager, you are responsible for establishing the *culturalising* rules of your eco-system. These rules create shared identity and shared vision. The eco-system level are outlined in Table 2.4.

Table 2.4 Eco-system level culturalising rules

Culturalising	Requirement	Eco-system level rule
	Shared identity	Who are we?
	Shared vision	Why are we here?

References

1. Van Der Hoorn B, Whitty SJ (2015) A Heideggerian paradigm for project management: breaking free of the disciplinary matrix and its Cartesian ontology. Int J Proj Manag 33(4):721–734
2. Drucker P (1985) Innovation and entrepreneurship: principles and practices. HarperTrade, New York
3. Anderson P (1999) Complexity theory and organization science. Organ Sci 10(3):216–232
4. Burnes B (2005) Complexity theories and organizational change. Int J Manage Rev 7(2):73–90
5. Hernes T (2003) Enabling and constraining properties of organizational boundaries. In: Managing boundaries in organizations: multiple perspectives. Springer, pp 35–54
6. Stacey RD (2007) Strategic management and organisational dynamics: the challenge of complexity to ways of thinking about organisations. Pearson Education
7. Stacey RD, Griffin D, Shaw P (2000) Complexity and management: fad or radical challenge to systems thinking? Psychology Press
8. Matinheikki J, Artto K, Peltokorpi A, Rajala R (2016) Managing inter-organizational networks for value creation in the front-end of projects. Int J Proj Manag 34(7):1226–1241
9. Matinheikki J, Pesonen T, Artto K, Peltokorpi A (2017) New value creation in business networks: the role of collective action in constructing system-level goals. Ind Mark Manag 67:122–133
10. Van der Borgh M, Cloodt M, Romme AGL (2012) Value creation by knowledge-based ecosystems: evidence from a field study. R&D Manag 42(2):150–169
11. Karrbom Gustavsson T (2013) Boundary spanning in construction projects: towards a model for managing efficient collaboration. In: 7th Nordic Conference on Construction Economics and Organization, Akademika Publishing
12. Asorey M, Ibort A, Marmo G (2005) Global theory of quantum boundary conditions and topology change. Int J Mod Phys A 20(5):1001–1025
13. Baggott JE (2011) The quantum story: a history in 40 moments. Oxford University Press
14. Chew WC (2012) Quantum mechanics made simple: lecture Notes. http://wcchew.ece.illinois.edu/chew/course/QMALL20121005.pdf
15. Reynolds CW (1987) Flocks, herds and schools: a distributed behavioral model. ACM SIGGRAPH Comput Graph 21(4):25–34
16. Toner J, Tu Y (1998) Flocks, herds, and schools: a quantitative theory of flocking. Phys Rev E 58(4):4828

17. Usher G (2019) Creating confidence amongst complexity: the 'lived experience' of client-side project managers in the Australian construction sector. Ph.D., Business and Management, University of Southern Queensland, Brisbane, Australia
18. Edvardsson B, Tronvoll B, Gruber T (2011) Expanding understanding of service exchange and value co-creation: a social construction approach. J Acad Mark Sci 39(2):327–339
19. Giddens A (1984) The constitution of society: outline of the theory of structuration. University of California Press
20. Giddens A (1979) Central problems in social theory: action, structure, and contradiction in social analysis. University of California Press
21. Edvardsson B, Skålén P, Tronvoll B (2012) Service systems as a foundation for resource integration and value co-creation. In: Special issue–Toward a better understanding of the role of value in markets and marketing. Emerald Group Publishing Limited, pp 79–126
22. Ecosystem Services (2019). http://www.teebweb.org/resources/ecosystem-services/
23. Usher G, Whitty SJ (2017) The final state convergence model. Int J Manag Proj Bus 10(4):770–795
24. Mayer BS (2015) The conflict paradox: seven dilemmas at the core of disputes. Wiley
25. Campbell S (2014) Conflict among team members can lead to better results. https://www.entrepreneur.com/article/238993
26. Estafanous J (2018) Why you need team conflict and how to make it productive. https://rallybright.com/why-your-team-needs-conflict-and-how-to-make-it-productive/
27. Thompson D. Quotes. (n.d) https://www.brainyquote.com/quotes/dorothy_thompson_135066#:~:text=Dorothy%20Thompson%20Quotes&text=Peace%20is%20not%20the%20absence%20of%20conflict%20but%20the%20presence,aggressive%20responses%2C%20alternatives%20to%20violence
28. R. E. Hill, "Managing interpersonal conflict in project teams," 1977 Massachusetts Institute of Techology, Sloan School of Management, Cambridge, Massachusetts.
29. Thamhain HJ, Wilemon DL (1975) Conflict management in project life cycles. Sloan Manag Rev 16(3):31
30. Tzu S (nd) The art of war. http://www.puppetpress.com/classics/ArtofWarbySunTzu.pdf
31. Greimas AJ, Courtés J, Rengstorf M (1989) The cognitive dimension of narrative discourse. New Literary History 20(3):563–579
32. Spee AP, Jarzabkowski P (2011) Strategic planning as communicative process. Organ Stud 32(9):29
33. Polletta F, Jasper JM (2001) Collective identity and social movements. Annu Rev Sociol 27(1):283–305
34. Van Stekelenburg J (2013) Collective identity. In: The Wiley-Blackwell encyclopedia of social and political movements. John Wiley & Son. Ltd Hoboken, New Jersey
35. Wasko MM, Faraj S (2005) Why should I share? Examining social capital and knowledge contribution in electronic networks of practice. MIS Q:35–57
36. Knox D, Ellis M, Speering R, Asvadurov S, Brinded T, Brown T (2017) The art of project leadership: delivering the world's largest projects. In: McKinsey capital projects and infrastructure practice. McKinsey & Co, Sydney, Australia, pp 1–72

What Is a Project?

Now that we have established that there is something that exists outside a project, I guess it's time to start having a look at the idea of what a project really is. You will recall that I have already debunked the ideas of 'unique' and 'temporary' as terms that should be incorporated into the definition of a project. So I guess I'd better come up with something new.

I'd like to do this by reframing the idea of a project using the ideas of Van der Hoorn and Whitty [1]. They have suggested a better way to understand whether an activity is a project or not is through the lens of competency.

What Is Competency?

Defining competency is not necessarily as straightforward as being competent or not being competent. There are, in fact, four levels of competency [2]. These are (1) unconscious incompetence, (2) conscious incompetence, (3) conscious competence and (4) unconscious competence. These four levels of competency are central to my new definition of projects, so let's have a look at them one at a time.

1. **Unconscious Incompetence**

   Unconscious incompetence is when an individual or organisation does not know that they don't know how to do something. They have no need of the skills they lack and therefore never contemplate acquiring or learning these skills.

   Unconscious incompetence is not necessarily a bad thing. There is a whole range of things in which I am unconsciously incompetent and completely happy to stay that way. Take sallikkattu (Indian bull wrestling) for example. I have no intention of ever learning how to do it nor can I ever envisage a scenario where I will need to know how to do it. I am completely ignorant of the competencies

© The Author(s), under exclusive license to Springer Nature Switzerland AG 2021
G. Usher, *Project Management in the 21st Century*, Management
for Professionals, https://doi.org/10.1007/978-3-030-71543-4_3

required to perform sallikkattu and quite happy in my ignorance, thank you very much.

2. **Conscious Incompetence**

   Conscious incompetence is when an individual or organisation knows they need to do something, but they don't know how to do it. Again, there is nothing wrong with being consciously incompetent. It simply means that there are things that need to be done that the individual or organisation doesn't necessarily want to learn how to do.

   For example, I once lived in a house where the sewer pipe got blocked and the toilet began to back up. At that point, I had a *very* definite need, but I also had no intention of learning the necessary skills to unblock the sewer. Instead, I just paid someone else to fix it while I went to the movies.

3. **Conscious Competence**

   Conscious competence is when an individual or organisation knows how to do something but preparing to do it and executing it is time-consuming, resource-intensive and requires a heavy conscious involvement.

   Reaching the level of conscious competence means that the individual or the organisation not only has a need, but they also think that investing the time and effort required to learn the skills will have long-term benefits. A good example of this is learning to drive a car. Driving is not the only solution to the problem of getting from one place to another; you also have Mum's taxi, Uber, public transport and walking. However, many of us invest the time and effort necessary to learn the competencies involved in driving because we want the benefits that come with having that competency.

4. **Unconscious Competence**

   Unconscious competence is when an individual or organisation has performed a skill so often that it has become 'second nature' and they can perform it almost without thinking about it.

Let's go back to the example of driving. If, like me, you have been driving for decades, then you probably find that you can get in a car and drive where you want to go without having to consciously think about things like pushing the accelerator to go faster or using the clutch to change gears. In fact, there are many times when I have gone on long road trips and never once thought about *how* to drive. This is because the competencies associated with driving have become so familiar to me, that I can perform it with my eyes closed (not literally, of course, I'm not an idiot).

Figure 3.1 shows how the four levels of the competence framework build on each other, and although these competencies are shown as a hierarchy, there are two very important points to remember. Firstly, none of these levels has a value judgement attached to them (i.e. no level is better or worse than the other), and, secondly, it is possible for an individual or an organisation to occupy all of the levels simultaneously (i.e. they might be unconsciously competent in one aspect, while unconsciously incompetent in another).

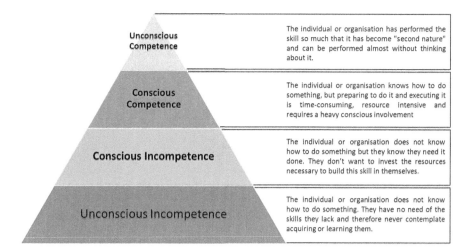

Fig. 3.1 The four-stage competency hierarchy

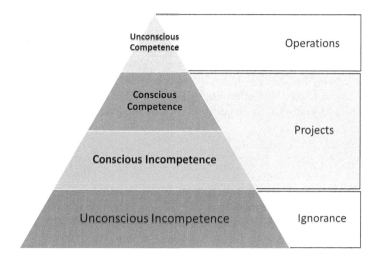

Fig. 3.2 Projects as defined by the competency model

To help us create a new definition for projects, I'm suggesting that a 'project' falls between the *unconscious* states.

If an individual or organisation is *unconsciously incompetent* about an activity, then they are in a state of *ignorance*. In other words, they do not need the competencies, so they don't even think about the competencies (remembering of course that in this case, 'ignorance' is not a bad thing, it is just a statement of competency). Conversely, if an individual or organisation is *unconsciously competent* when performing an activity, then we can say that it is just part of their normal *operations*. That is to say that they don't need to think about completing the activity; they just get in and do it. Therefore, I'm suggesting that any activity, task or action in which an individual or organisation is *conscious* of their level of competency should be considered a project (see Fig. 3.2).

Using this competency-based lens, a project is defined not by the product, service or result that it produces (® does) but by whether a person or organisation are conscious of needing to undertake certain activities. In other words, a project is not something that they can ignore nor is it something they can do with their eyes shut. Projects require the parties involved to be consciously engaging in the process.

So, how does my new definition of project work in a real situation? Let me explain by asking you a simple question. *Is playing a song on a guitar a project?*

If you use the PMBoK® definition, the answer will come down to whether you or anyone else, has played this piece of music before. If the answer is no, then its unique and temporary, and you have a project. If the answer is yes, then although it might be temporary, it is not unique and therefore can't be a project.

However, if you use a competency-based definition, the answer is not clear-cut. Although the end product (the song) might have been played thousands of times before by other musicians, that doesn't necessarily disqualify the activity from being a 'project'. Using our competency-based classification, if I am an accomplished musician who plays my guitar 8 h a day, 7 days a week, then it's not difficult for me to play the song—in fact, I can probably do it without really thinking about what I'm doing. In this case, playing the song is not a project.

However, if I am only just learning the guitar, I will need to invest much more time and effort to get the same result. In this case, for me, the activity is a project. The end result hasn't changed, the song still gets played, but the level of competency surrounding the delivery of the outcome is different. In this case, playing this song on the guitar could either be classified as 'operations' (if I can do it without really thinking about it) or as 'project' (if it requires conscious effort and planning to achieve).

So, using this new definition, we see that it is the *competency level* of the person or organisation doing the work that determines whether the activity is a project, not the inherent uniqueness or temporariness of the activity.

Now, this is where things get interesting.

It is conceivable that if I practice the song enough, the activity that used to be a 'project' could reach the point where it is no longer classified as a 'project' (by me) because I have become *unconsciously competent* in delivering the outcome. Or conversely, an activity in which I was *unconsciously competent* yesterday (playing a song on my guitar) could become a project tomorrow (i.e. say someone asks me to play the same song using a left-handed guitar). Once again, no change to the outcome required, but a significant change in terms of the competencies required.

Based on this, I'd like to propose that a project is:

Any activity in which an individual or organisation must be conscious of their competency to achieve the intended outcome.

While you are trying that on for size, I'd also like to point out that this definition also helps explain a couple of other phenomena in the project management space.

First, it provides a delineation between project managers who are employed within an organisation and those who are project management consultants.

We have already discussed that the defining attribute between *conscious incompetence* and *conscious competence* is whether an organisation wants to invest the time and effort required to learn the skills necessary to fulfil their need so those skills can provide long-term benefits. If an organisation believes that they need those skills long term, they will develop their competency in that area. In the case of organisations, they may regularly need to deliver projects to keep their operations running (i.e. building factories to manufacture products). Building the factory is a project, and manufacturing products in that factory is operations. If the organisation is doing enough projects, it may make sense for them to develop this competency internally. Although the organisation now has this competency, because every factory is different, they will never reach the level of *unconscious competency*. They can deliver their own projects, but doing so will always be an activity in which they need to remain *consciously competent*.

On the other hand, the same organisation might decide that they need the factories, but they don't feel the need to have the competencies required to manage the design and construction of these factories themselves. In other words, they decide to remain *consciously incompetent*. So, how do they get that need fulfilled? They outsource that competency to another person or organisation, like a consultant project manager (not unlike me paying the plumber and then heading off to the movies).

Thus, we see that the competency-based model for project management also provides a clear delineation between the roles of the employed project manager and the consultant project manager (Fig. 3.3).

Second, our new definition of a 'project' provides a foundation for understanding the process of value co-creation within projects. For value to be created, according to our phenomenological definition, you need to be conscious of what you are experiencing. You can't create value in the unconscious states because you are unaware

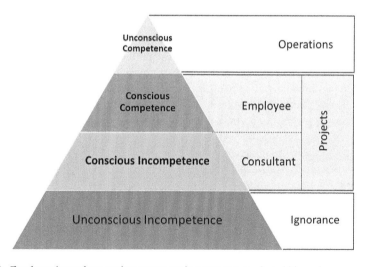

Fig. 3.3 Employee/consultant project managers in a competency-based hierarchy

of what you are doing. Value is created by being actively involved in the process of delivering a project.

Ok, now that we have a new definition for projects, let's have a look at what this means in terms of managing them.

Managing Projects

Let's return to the project eco-system and order-generating rules for a moment. As you will no doubt recall, the project eco-system develops around the project. This eco-system is a complex adaptive system that needs to operate at the edge of chaos at the system level but requires order at the project level. This allows the system to stave off entropy while ensuring that it is constrained enough not to fly apart.

The eco-system level rules are designed to promote dynamic freedom by ensuring the system has broad rules. However, things are very different at the project level. At this level projects need structure and control, so more prescriptive rules are required.

The idea of applying different rules at different levels of a system may seem contradictory. But our entire universe is premised on this exact phenomenon. If we view the universe at a macro-level, we can use classic mechanics to understand and predict things like the trajectory of planets or the impacts of gravity on a given body. That's because, at the macro-level, the universe runs according to deterministic laws.

However, if you view our universe at the sub-atomic level, all those deterministic laws break down and everything runs completely contradictory to classical, Newtonian mechanics. Quantum mechanics demonstrates that at the sub-atomic level, the four kinematic properties of mass (m), position (r), velocity (v) and acceleration (a) no longer work the way we would expect them to, based on classic mechanics [3]. This is because our sub-atomic universe is governed by a completely different set of rules to our macro-universe.

In short, classical mechanics is based on the assumption that any dynamic variable can be measured with arbitrary precision and without interference from other measurements. However, quantum mechanics demonstrates that the process of measuring a variable at the sub-atomic level may physically impact the whole system, thereby preventing us from knowing what would have occurred if we didn't undertake the measurement process [4–6].

The same apparent contradiction occurs when we view either the project eco-system or the project. At the system level, we want broad rules which create the freedom to boundary span and self-organise. But at the project level, we want prescriptive rules to allow us to plan, monitor and manage the outcome of our project.

The order-generating rules at both the eco-system level and the project level can be grouped into the same categories: provisioning, regulating, supporting and culturalising. However, these groups of rules serve different purposes at the different levels. So, let's have a look at these project-level, order-generating rules one by one.

Project-Level Provisioning Rules

At a project level, our role is to ensure that the project is adequately provisioned so it can achieve its stated goal. We need to ensure that we have enough of the right resources set aside, or at least ready to be procured at the right time, so that we can successfully manage the project through to completion.

Broadly, there are seven categories of provisions that you need to prepare for at the project level. These are:

1. Time.
2. Materials.
3. Finances.
4. Legal.
5. Environmental.
6. Technology.
7. Workforce.

For the project to be completed, each of these categories must have sufficient depth and availability to meet the project's specific needs at the time that they are needed.

So, the first project-level provisioning rule is to make sure you are addressing all seven provisioning categories within your project. However, that's not as simple as it sounds

'It didn't sound simple' I can hear you say. To which I would respond 'Yes, but you are yet to appreciate how not simple it isn't'. Or something like that.

If project-level provisioning was as simple as just making sure you had enough resources available in each of these seven categories, then project management would be a breeze. What makes life is difficult is that all seven of these categories impact one another, and somewhere within these seven categories of provisions, there is one to which all others are subordinate.

Can you guess which one it is?

One Provision to Rule Them All...

Ok, ok, that was a trick question. While it's true that there is a single dominant category of provisioning required for your project, it's not always the same one for every project. That's why things get complicated. When you first kick off your project, you haven't been exposed to the most difficult element of project-level provisioning, which is *managing constraints.*

Constraints can be thought of as the relationship that exists between the provisioning categories and their combined relationship to the project. Although all seven categories of provision are required in each project, this doesn't mean that they are required equally or that they are the same every time. Within this list of categories, there will be one provisioning category that will be a bottleneck for the whole project, and it's part of our job to identify that constraint and to plan everything else around it.

I want you to imagine that your project is a container which can only be filled to the brim when the contents of seven smaller containers (the provisioning areas) are completely emptied into it. For our explanation, I want you to assume that these seven smaller containers are not equal in size but at the start of the process each one is adequately provisioned with sufficient liquid to fill your 'project container'. Now imagine that the seven smaller containers are interconnected. Each one pours into another, then into another, and so on until the liquid in the seven smaller containers is discharged into the larger *project container* and the process is complete. Figure 3.4 shows you what I mean.

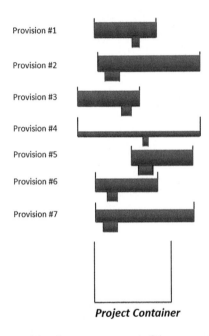

Fig. 3.4 The provisioning model at the commencement of the process (t_0)

Looking at this model, do you think that the project container at the bottom will be successfully filled to the brim, once all the liquid is discharged?

The answer is 'No' and here's why. If we were to take a snapshot of the process after it has been running for some time, it would look like this (Fig. 3.5):

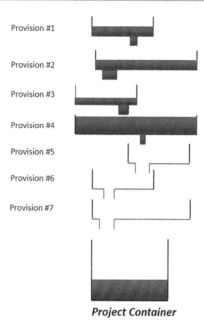

Fig. 3.5 The provisioning model at a specific time in the process (t_n)

The reason the container hasn't filled has nothing to do with the inadequate provisioning at the commencement of the process. Instead, it has to do with a single, dominant constraint within the process that bottlenecks everything else 'upstream' while simultaneously starving everything else 'downstream' (Fig. 3.6).

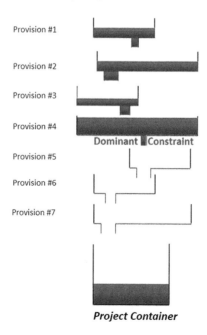

Fig. 3.6 The impact of the dominant constraint

The ability of a single constraint to completely dictate the successful completion of the project is the central theme in Goldratt's Theory of Constraints [7]. Because the seven provisioning categories are interrelated (e.g. time delays impact costs, the ability to access a workforce is governed by legal arrangements, the progress of the workforce is dependent on the materials, etc.), there will always be one constraint that dominates the overall progress of the project, and it's our job to work out what that constraint is and then manage the rest of the project around it.

Overcoming Constraints by Building in Safety Margins: A Recipe for Failure

So, let's say you've worked out what the dominant constraint is. Your next step has to be mitigating the impacts of that constraint. One of the most common ways that we try to manage project constraints is by building safety margins into that particular provision. At first glance, the idea of building in safety margins appears to be a prudent thing to do. However, there is a growing body of research that indicates our predilection for including safety margins in our projects could be the main reason that so many projects fail. And here's why.

Imagine you have a project in which you have identified that time is the dominant constraint. Your project is simple, but because you know time is the dominant constraint, you also know that you better get the programming right. So, you engage a professional scheduler.

Your scheduler documents all the tasks required to complete the project and assigns each of them an estimated duration. In theory, this should give you a fairly good idea of the duration of your project. However, because the scheduler's professional reputation is built on ensuring projects are completed within the schedule that she has developed, she protects her reputation by including a little extra time into each task. She includes this *safety margin* because she is painfully aware that the duration of some of the tasks are based entirely on her best professional guess. So, including a little extra time in some of the tasks seems the sensible thing to do. You know, just to be sure. She then provides this schedule to you as the project manager.

Now, because you have responsibility for delivering the project according to this program and you know that time is your dominant constraint, you will most likely review the schedule. Being a seasoned professional, you know the sorts of things that can go wrong on a project. So, before you agree to take on the project, you add a little more time into each of the tasks that you think could be a risk. This is your *safety margin*, and you want it built in because it seems to be the sensible thing to do. You know, just to be sure. You then pass your revised schedule up to the sponsor for endorsement.

Your sponsor probably answers to a senior executive or a board. There is no way she wants to report that her project is failing in terms of the time commitment. So, what does she do? You guessed it—she adds in a *safety margin* because it seems to be the sensible thing to do. You know, just to be sure.

Can you guess what the impact of this compounding safety margins is on your time provisioning for this project? Well, recent research by Izmailov, Korneva and Kozhemiakin [8] suggests that, if a project has three layers of safety margin incorporated (like our example), the entire project duration can be inflated by as much as 60% over what the project actually requires for successful completion. Now, you won't be able to find this safety margin of course because it's hidden within the time estimation of individual tasks. What it does mean, however, is that your project is now over-provisioned up the wahzoo in terms of time.

So, with all this extra time built in, you would think that this project is almost guaranteed to be completed within the allocated time, right?

Nope!

According to the same study, only 44% of projects that have safety margins factored into the individual tasks will finish on time, and to do this, 70% of those projects will reduce the amount of work originally planned. So how the hell can a project that is 60% over-provisioned for time still fail to meet the forecast date for completion?

Well, the answer is quite simple really. Despite all compounding safety margins included within the individual tasks, you have forgotten one thing—human nature.

As we have explored throughout this book, the traditional, hard-paradigm reductionist tools and techniques of project management cannot be extricated from the quirks of human nature, and provisioning at the project level is no exception.

In the case of 'time', there are two particular idiosyncrasies of human nature that will almost guarantee that, even a project with as much as 60% safety margin, it will still run overtime. These two quirks are known as (1) student's syndrome and (2) Parkinson's law. Student syndrome consumes safety margin before a task starts, and Parkinson's law consumes all remaining safety margin at the end of the task.

Student syndrome is the observed phenomenon in which people only fully engage with a task at the last possible moment before a deadline. This is particularly true if a person is extremely busy or working on multiple tasks or projects. What happens is the person responsible for the task will make their own assessment of how long the task will take with almost complete disregard for how much time is actually allocated for that task in the schedule. If they believe they have more time available than the task requires, they will use this excess time to complete other tasks that are already behind schedule before starting this one. Although the idea of delaying the start of a new task that appears to have loads of time available, in order to complete other tasks that are already behind, seems logical, the impact on the project schedule can be devastating. Can you see why? Because the safety margin that was intended to be used at the end of the task (if it was needed) was consumed before the task even commenced. This means that any actual delay to the task will still cause the task to overrun the safety-margin-laden time allocation.

The second quirk stems from the fact there is no real incentive for the people doing the task to complete it early. Parkinson's law is the observation that 'work expands to fill all the time remaining for its completion'. Parkinson's law will impact a project for two reasons. Firstly, it's in every person's best interest to make sure that they always look busy, even if that means doing work that might not be critical to the completion of the task. We do this to protect our future safety margins. If we finish this task too early, we might find that the scheduler reduces the time allocated to it in the next schedule. If that happens, and we run into obstacles next time, we might end up facing some sort of penalty for taking too long. So, we protect the safety margin against future removal by using all time we have been given, even if that time is way too long for the particular job. Secondly, because we instinctively believe we are more likely to be reprimanded for poor-quality work than we are to be rewarded for early completion, we will use any spare time available, after we have finished the job, to 'polish' or 'improve' the final product before handing it over.

The existence of these two idiosyncrasies of human nature means that regardless how much safety margin you build into the schedule, you can almost guarantee it will not only be completely consumed but that any obstacles or challenges faced will still delay the project.

The simple fact is that, regardless of how much safety margin you build into any one of the seven provisioning categories, there is a prevailing human trait that will erode it before it's actually needed. Do you have extra cash in the budget? Great! Let's gold plate these doo-dads, because that really should have been included in the original budget. Do you have extra materials on site? Fantastic! Then I can speed up because I don't have to be quite so worried about reducing wastage. Do we have more workforce on site than we need? Awesome! Let's get three people holding that ladder instead of one, just to be sure.

The simple fact is we can't manage constraints by building in safety margins. If people think they have more provisions than they need, they will find a way to use that to their benefit, which, of course, only serves to erode that safety margin away before it does its job.

So, how do we overcome this?

Provisioning and Constraint Management Through Buffers

One solution is to provision your project using the principle of buffering. Goldratt suggested that the only way to truly manage constraints is to remove all the hidden safety margins and strip everything back to the bare necessity to complete each task [7]. Then, once all the safety margins are removed, you add in buffers, as a completely separate provision. Goldratt suggested several different types of buffers, project buffers, feeder buffers and resource buffers [8]. These buffers are stand-alone blocks of provisions that can be drawn on, if and when needed.

Extracting the safety margins from individual provision 'containers' and including them as discrete packages ensures that they are separated, visible and not squandered. If the provisions included in these buffers are not required, they are retired, released or returned.

Using buffers at the project level ensures you have much better control over what provisions are being used and when. You will know exactly how much extra you have of each provision at any point in time, and you will ensure that the project is running as lean as possible. Creating buffers also overcomes the complex issue of constraint interdependencies. It gives you greater control over your provisions. It highlights for future projects where the trouble spots are. It allows you to test and validate what provisions are required for your project, and it overcomes the impacts of provisioning relationships and constraints that you could not have foreseen when you commenced the project.

Summary

In terms of the project-level provisioning, your role is to ensure that there are sufficient resources to complete the project. Achieving this is not simply a function of ensuring there are ample supplies available. You also need to identify the dominant constraint and successfully manage it. To achieve all this, you need to put the project-level provisioning rules in place (Table 3.1).

Table 3.1 Project-level provisioning rules

Provisioning	Requirement	Project-level provisioning rule
	Ample supply	Make sure all seven categories are adequately provisioned
	Managing constraints	Identify the one constraint that overrides everything else
	Buffering	Use buffers rather than safety margins to manage constraints

Project-Level Regulating Rules

At the project-level, four regulating rules promote order generation. These have to do with (1) planning, (2) monitoring, (3) controlling and (4) discipline. If you have been a project manager for any length of time, I would expect that you have encountered and developed your own rules in these areas, but perhaps you were not aware that you were doing it, or why it needed to be done. So, let's have a look at these rules in a little more detail.

Planning

The idea that project managers plan things is almost axiomatic. To paraphrase a Facebook meme, 'One does not simply just 'do' a project'. Project managers create plans for everything. Because of this, you might be tempted to think that plans (i.e. project plans, programs, schedules, etc.) are the project-level, regulating rules. Well, if you think that, then congratulations, you are completely wrong.

First things first, you need to understand that plans are basically useless—but creating them is extremely important.

As a project manager, the process of creating plans for a project has always bugged me. I couldn't understand why I needed to draft out detailed plans to deliver a project that was delivered in a dynamic environment and could be impacted by unexpected influences that are outside my control at any moment.

Understanding exactly why project managers kept 'planning' became one of the central themes in my PhD thesis [10]. In my research, I found that every single one of the project managers I interviewed created detailed plans for delivering their projects. These plans map out the steps they would take from the day that the project was assigned to them through to the end of the defects liability period. I also asked these same project managers if these detailed plans ever needed to be changed during the project delivery process. They all said pretty much the same thing: 'Only, all the time'.

So, this idea of creating plans became a bit of a bugbear for me. I knew we all did it, but at the same time, it seemed rather pointless to create detailed plans for the project, only to go changing them every other day. Then one day, as I was developing a new planning methodology for use in the construction sector [11], it finally dawned on me why we plan out projects. Are you ready for this?

We do it because it makes everyone involved with the project *feel better*.

That was my epiphany. Pretty much the only reason why we go to the effort of planning out something that we know will need to be changed tomorrow is because everyone *feels* more confident when they think there is something 'solid' to hang on to. When I realised this the lightbulb went on, and I understood President Eisenhower statement—'...plans are useless. But planning is indispensable...'.

This idea that our plans are useless is extremely important for project managers. One of the most dangerous things we can do is to believe that the plan we put together at the start is the way the project actually needs to be delivered. The sooner we realise that our plans, no matter how well-thought-out and detailed, can be overturned in an instant, the sooner we can begin to see them for what they are—*tools that create confidence*. Our plans are value-creating artefacts, not instruction manuals. Plans and schedules are documents that help everyone relax a little because they feel like they know what's going on, and this sense of confidence is essential for moving forward. Without documents like project plans and schedules, the entire project team would wander around in a fog of confusion, never sure how to get started or what step they should take next.

Grasping this was a turning point in my career. I realised that it is the act of planning, not the plans themselves, that is important. The act of planning helps us regulate the project by having, at the very least, one viable way to move forward. The process of planning forces us to think about how to go about doing something. Planning demands conscious effort. However, everything we do after that in terms of documenting that plan is almost completely pointless.

That's why, every time new information is provided to us, we need to go back to the planning process. Sure, we might then go and create a new plan, but if you think about it, this has more to do with creating confidence for ourselves and others that we at least have some idea of how we are going to keep moving towards the end goal.

This is incredibly liberating for a project manager because now, rather than having to develop up the *right* plan at the start of the project, you just need to develop a *reasonable* plan and get moving. There is no need to apologise or feel like you are not a good project manager if the plan changes. After all, it was only ever just one way of doing the job. When you get new information, or something comes up that you couldn't have foreseen, you don't stress about what that means for the plan— you just make a new one.

So, in terms of the project-level order-generating rules, this one is simple. Don't worry about the plans, but always keep planning. Be ready to absorb new information and respond to this by planning again. You regulate the project, not by creating the perfect plan at the beginning, but by responding swiftly and pragmatically to new information. Rather than trying to adopt the production management idea of creating the one, non-varying, repeatable, scientifically determined plan for your project, you just plan for what is known, have some ideas up your sleeve for the unknowns and keep moving forward.

This leads us to our first project-level regulating rule: *Plans are useless but keep planning*.

Monitoring

Monitoring progress is a critical aspect of managing a project.

I know, I know. I just finished telling you that plans are useless, and now I'm telling you that you should be monitoring them. I mean why should you even bother monitoring time, cost and quality when you know that things will change? Well, the answer is twofold.

First, monitoring improves performance. For some reason, which scientists are yet to explain, we all behave better when we think someone is watching us. Back in 1976, a group of researchers did an interesting experiment. It was Halloween in America, and when the young trick-or-treaters came to the door of one house, a researcher opened the door holding a bowl of candy. The research team then arranged for the phone to ring. The researcher at the door said to the children 'I have to answer that, please help yourself, but only take one piece each'. With that, the researcher left the bowl on the doorstep and walked inside to get the phone. The research team did this experiment twice, but they changed one important variable.

In the first experiment, when the door was opened, the children could only see the wall inside the house. For the second experiment, a mirror was hung on the wall, so the children could see their reflections as they took candy from the bowl. The results were amazing. When the children faced a blank wall, 28.5% of them took more than one piece of candy. When the mirror was in place, and the children could see their reflection, only 14.5% of them took more than one piece of candy. The researchers surmised that the children behaved better when they 'felt' they were being watched. Just the feeling that someone was watching them, even though it was their own reflections, reduced the chances of breaking the 'rules' by almost 50% [12].

The simple fact is we all behave better when we think someone is watching us. We tend to be more productive, more efficient and more engaged. This is why you need to monitor the progress of your projects. You don't monitor to control; you monitor to improve performance. It's like Peter Drucker said, '…what gets measured, gets managed…' [13].

Second, monitoring allows you to continually run project diagnostics. I'm going to let you in on another little secret. Although project managers do a lot of planning, most of the time we don't really know what's going to happen—we just make it look like we do. This illusion of being in control of the project is possible because we are constantly monitoring the project against a range of indicators. The ones that we are most familiar with are time, cost and quality, but they aren't the only ones. We are also monitoring the environment for potential risks and opportunities, the alignment between the project reality and the project members' expectations, supply and logistics, political stability, etc.

Monitoring our project against pre-established indicators allows us to see issues and trends early. Savvy project managers can then use this information to make any necessary adjustments to either (a) bring the project back in line with the original plan or (b) adjust the expectations of the people involved with the project [14, 15].

I often tell my senior project staff that they don't need to know the entire project plan, they only need specific detail for about 2 months ahead of where they are now and then a broad outline of how to move forward after that (these timelines could be different for different sectors but the principle is the same). The key thing is making sure that you are monitoring a few key indicators on your project so that you can see any deviations from your current plans or trends that might be developing before anyone else does. That way you have the information you need to either fine-tune the project, change the plan or change people's expectations of what is going to happen before anyone else realises what's going on. This gives us project-regulating rule number two: *measure performance to run diagnostics*.

Controlling

Controlling a project requires a project manager perpetrate a particularly important illusion. This illusion has two parts, and you need to understand how both parts work to pull this trick off.

The first thing you need to know about controlling any project is that you can't actually do it. Over my career, I have watched good project managers burn themselves out labouring under the false belief that their role is to control their project. Projects are complex activities undertaken in dynamic environments. Projects have interdependent variables that impact their progress and efficiency, and many of these variables are outside the project manager's sphere of influence. This level of complexity and dynamism means that it is impossible for anyone to actually *control* a project. If anyone tells you differently, they are either suffering from delusions of grandeur regarding their abilities or they have not had enough experience delivering projects yet.

The second part of the control illusion is that everyone else involved in the project desperately wants to *think* that you are in control. One of the striking things that came out of my PhD research was that the people involved in the project, especially the ones who had never been involved with a project before, are afraid. They won't tell you that outright, but they are afraid because they have been made responsible for delivering this complex beast without any real understanding of how it works or what should be done. They have conscious incompetence. So, the one thing they need from a project manager more than having a 'certified practitioner' or 'technical expert' is someone who gives them confidence that everything is under control.

Now don't get me wrong, I am a big fan of certification and technical expertise. But in my opinion, their power derives from being a quick way to create confidence in your ability to deliver the project more than anything else. But that's a topic for another day.

Returning to the illusion that you must perform; it is simply this—always look like you are in control. This illusion is a necessary confidence trick. It provides the freedom we need to get the project underway and to keep it moving forward. If the others involved with the project are not fooled by the illusion, then prepare yourself for some very trying times. Every decision you need to make will be scrutinised. You will find yourself needing to prepare detailed decision brief and option papers. You will spend countless hours justifying why the most basic actions need to be taken. Trust me when I tell you, not pulling off this illusion is no fun. It makes delivering the project a long, hard road.

The encouraging part, however, is that for the most part, everyone involved in the project wants to believe the illusion. Most of them know that if they were to look hard at your magic trick, they would see how it's done. Because they know this, most of the time they don't look for fear of seeing what's really going on.

Research by Soderholm [14] and Usher and Whitty [15] suggest the illusion works something like this. You set the scene for the illusion by creating detailed plans of how the project *could* be achieved (these are usually time, cost and risk-based plans). You then closely monitor the project against those plans so you can identify trends, risks and opportunities before anyone else. If you see any deviations from your plans, you first try to correct them yourself (quietly), and if you can't, you begin to prepare everyone involved in the project for changes to the plans well in advance of actually having to action the changes. For their part, the 'audience' allow the illusion to work because (1) they desperately want someone to be in control and (2) they have no idea themselves what to do to keep the project running.

All of this gives us the basis for our project-level, order-generating rule: *Always maintain the illusion of control.*

Discipline

Throughout this book, I have tried to convey that one of the most important things that you can do as a project manager is to create a sense of confidence for everyone involved with the project. This sense of confidence comes from making people feel like the project is being managed and that the required result can be achieved.

But how do we create this sense of confidence when we know that every project is an unwieldy beast which resists being controlled? Well, quite simply, we use a framework of discipline.

The word 'discipline' can have several different definitions. In terms of the role that it plays in creating project-level, order-generating rules, I am going to use two of these definitions. The first definition considers discipline as the act of behaving in a measured way. The second definition considers discipline to be the process of training others to act according to a certain code of behaviour using both rewards and punishment.

Definition 1: Behaving in a Measured Way

We've just finished looking at why I think it is impossible for you to 'control' your project. However, I don't believe that this gives you a hall pass to behave in a haphazard or shabby way.

As we discussed projects are?', complex dynamic systems which are most efficient when they operate at the edge of chaos. At the project level, chaos is created through the dynamic environment, unknown unknowns and the people who are involved with the project. However, this chaos needs a balancing force so that it doesn't degenerate. This order must be created and modelled by you.

Project managers do this by adopting familiar methodologies and applying these to their projects. These methodologies include PMBoK®, PRINCE2® or Agile. These methodologies are the only tools we have available to us to balance the uncertainty and dynamism of our projects.

Applying these methodologies is the discipline of project management. These methodologies create a framework for controlled behaviour where there would otherwise be none. Applying formal methodologies to a project serves two main purposes.

First and foremost, it gives you a broad plan of how to get started and how to keep progressing. This is very similar to the concept we discussed about the difference between plans and planning. Having this framework means that you don't have to work with a blank canvas. When you start the project, or when you get stuck on the way through, you can use these methodologies to help guide you forward.

Applying these methodologies (whichever one best suits your project) allows you to model the controlled behaviour that others need to see. The framework provides the discipline that people need to create a sense of confidence that everything is OK. Making sure you have a clear project charter; ensuring that registers, meetings and WBS are developed; preparing meeting agendas; taking minutes; and following up on action items are all part of the discipline of project management. It is you creating order amidst chaos, by clearly outlining what you are going to do and then making sure you do it. You must discipline yourself to model the behaviour you want others to emulate. To do this, you need to approach your project in a disciplined way and maintain that discipline throughout the life of your project.

Definition 2: Training Others to Act According to a Certain Code of Behaviour

This second definition has to do with training others to act a certain way using both rewards and punishment. Initially, you might not feel comfortable with the idea of using rewards and punishments to discipline grown adults to make them do their jobs. However, if you have ever managed a project before, I suspect you are already quite adept at it.

Let's look at the concept of 'formal' reward and punishment. One of the most common forms of formal discipline (i.e. making others behave according to a code of conduct) is a contract. Essentially, a contract is a written agreement that codifies behaviour. Sure, it outlines what must be done, but mostly it outlines the acceptable behaviours of each party as they work together towards achieving a common outcome. This is why contracts say things like '…The Principal must…' and '…The Contractor shall…'. These terms explicitly outline the behaviour that is expected of the parties. If you have ever had to administer a contract (e.g. approving or rejecting some sort of claim), then you have already been through the process of either rewarding (e.g. making sure they get paid) or punishing (e.g. denying a claim for failure to comply with the conditions of a contract).

However, project managers also use more informal means of discipline to train people. We do this in a multitude of ways. Let me give you some examples. My office at work uses an 'open plan' arrangement. This means that I get to hear up to 60 project managers a day, 'disciplining' their project team members or stakeholders to get the behaviour they desire.

This morning I overheard one senior project manager explaining to an engineer that the submitted report needs to be redone because it lacked clarity on the key points and was not in accordance with the format that everyone agreed to. I heard another senior project manager explaining to a sponsor that any changes the sponsor wanted to make needs to go through her as the project manager, in writing, and that the sponsor can't just go on-site and direct changes to the building. I heard an assistant project manager on the phone to an architect following up on some overdue action items from a previous meeting and explaining that if the plans weren't provided by Friday that she would have no choice but to let the sponsor know that the delay was the architect's fault.

All of these are examples of project managers disciplining others to get the behaviour they desire. In these informal interactions, the rewards and punishments can be as simple as words of praise, rejection of poor-quality work or threats of escalation. All of these, and many more, form part of your arsenal of behaviour-modifying tools.

When it comes to the project-level order-generating rules, you have two aspects of discipline to consider. The first is how you behave personally, and the second is how you train everyone else to conform to the behaviour you require. Our regulations project-level, order-generating rule is: *Model and enforce the desired behaviours.*

Summary

In terms of these project-level regulating rules, your role is to plan, monitor, control and maintain discipline. The project-level regulating rules are outlined in Table 3.2.

Table 3.2 Project-level regulating rules

Regulating	Requirement	Project-level rule
	Planning	Plans are useless but keep planning
	Monitoring	Measure performance to run diagnostics
	Controlling	Always maintain the illusion of control
	Discipline	Model and enforce the desired behaviours

Project-Level Supporting Rules

> *When it comes to managing a project, one of the easiest tasks is meeting the expectations of*
> *all stakeholders. This is because there is only one expectation that needs to be met and*
> *everyone is crystal clear on what that is.*
>
> (No project manager, ever.)

Expectation Management

In my PhD research, I looked at the role that stakeholder's expectations had on our ability to deliver a successful project [10, 15–17]. What I discovered is 'expectations' are one of the most influential criteria in whether people involved with the project are satisfied with the project's outcomes. My research explored how project 'success' and stakeholder 'satisfaction' are two completely different phenomena, and while we might think that delivering a 'successful' project ensures stakeholder 'satisfaction', the truth is that there is only a weak correlation between the two. I also found that making sure stakeholders 'felt satisfied' with their experience of the project management journey was more important than making sure the project was a 'success' when measured against traditional critical success factors.

The idea that delivering a 'successful' project can lead to leave stakeholder's 'dissatisfied' or that a 'failed' project can leave stakeholders 'satisfied' is a paradox that is fundamental to the concept of value co-creation. The relationship that creates this dichotomy is an extremely complex one, but in a nutshell, the problem arises because traditional project management theory fails to address the human side of projects [18, 19]. For seven decades, we have convinced ourselves, and everyone else, that our primary role is to ensure our project delivers the required scope on time and under budget. We then went about convincing ourselves this was the same thing as fulfilling everyone's expectations about the project.

Epic fail!

The problem is that a project delivers a *thing,* but that thing is delivered *for* people—and people are complex beings who often have strange, subconscious, emotional-fuelled reasons for behaving the way they do. To make matters worse, delivering a project usually involves working with more than one of these complex creatures. A project usually has groups of different people working together. Each of these people will have their own drivers for satisfaction, and there is no guarantee that any of their expectations align with the realities of the project.

Mark Manson highlights that '…Experiences generate emotions. Emotions generate values. Values generate narratives of meaning…' [20]. What he is saying is that our experiences create meaning in our lives. This is true of everything we do, and delivering projects is no exception. Because of this, I believe one of the most important project management tasks is choreographing people's experiences so that they align with the realities of the project.

Achieving this is no easy task, but the fundamental principle for doing this never changes. You align the project delivery with people's expectations, not by changing the project but by changing people's expectations.

At the project level, you are attempting to get everyone's expectations aligned with what is happening now *and* what you see coming down the track. This is a utopian aspiration of course, but we must have something to aim for. Getting everyone's expectations aligned with the realities of the project is not always possible, but at the very least, you need to ensure you have adjusted the expectations of the key decision-makers so that what you believe will happen is what they expect to experience.

There are many techniques for expectation management, but one of my favourites is an adaptation of Aristotle's advice for public speaking, and it goes like this 'Tell people what you are going to tell them, tell them, then tell them what you told them'.

The simple fact is most people are unaware of their emotional drivers [20]. This provides you with an opportunity to condition and ultimately change people's emotional drivers by easing them into ideas.

Active expectation management is one occasion where confirmation bias works in your favour. Evolution has taught humans to fear what we don't understand, but when we are exposed to the idea of potentially dangerous or undesirable events before they happen, we tend to expend most of our emotional energy associated with that event before the event happens. This practice of preconditioning the psyche for unpleasant events is a core principle of Stoicism. Fundamentally, the practice is premised on the idea that by spending time thinking about a dangerous or undesirable event before it occurs, our subconscious has time to accept ideas that it might otherwise reject as unpalatable.

As a savvy project manager, you can use this to your advantage. By broadcasting unpalatable news well in advance of its occurrence, you can slowly and almost imperceptibly align people's expectations to what you think is going to happen. If you do this delicately and tactfully, you can often have them believe they were the ones who foresaw the event in the first place. This can give them an ironic sense of satisfaction when an unsavoury but inevitable event does occur, because it validates their keen foresight about the project.

Knowing this provides us with our first, project-level supporting rule. *Expectations are flexible, so bend them.*

Sense-Making

Human beings are driven by the need to make sense of their experiences. Everything we understand, believe or value in our existence is a result of some string of experiences that we have arbitrarily connected in our minds in order make sense of our lives [21, 22]. This instinctual need to understand how everything *fits together* presents, in my opinion, one of the most under-appreciated and under-utilised tools in the project manager's repertoire. The ability to create their own narrative for the project [20].

The first thing you need to understand about sense-making is that all experiences are value agnostic. That is, in themselves, they have no value. We assign value to our experiences, and from that, we determine whether the experience is a 'good experience' or a 'bad experience'. What's more, the meaning that we make of our experiences can change over time. As Sigmund Freud once said, '…One day, in retrospect, the years of struggle will strike you as the most beautiful…'.

Understanding that value is *assigned* to an experience rather than being an *inherent attribute* of the experience itself provides us with an opportunity to make sense of our project experiences so that the value we want is assigned to them. Let me give you an example.

Let's assume you have just received an email from the contractor in which they tell you that they have found a mistake in fire services plans. This mistake will push back the completion date by 1 month and add an extra $60,000 to the project cost. Being a project manager who understands the importance of sense-making, you ask the contractor how long and how much it would have taken to rectify the problem if the problem was discovered after the building was completed. The contractor explains that if the error was found after all the other services and ceiling linings were installed, it could take up to 3 months to rectify the fault. This would undoubtedly result in hundreds of thousands of dollars in lost production time and abortive works. So you say to yourself, 'Happy Days'.

This additional information gives you everything you need to turn this new information into a 'good experience', and it all comes down to how you chose to make sense of what just happened.

One option is to call a project meeting and tell everyone 'I've just found out about a delay on the project's critical path. As a result of [*insert scapegoat's name here*]'s mistake, we will now be one month behind schedule, and the whole project will end up costing $60,000 more than we had budgeted'.

What do you think happens when you present the information like this? Most likely, vast amounts of time and effort will be expended by the nominated scapegoat to prove that the mistake was a result of someone else's error or omission. This path creates a breakdown in relationship and trust. It perpetuates a move towards adversarial contract administration and generally sends the message that someone has failed. Let's call this the 'bad experience'.

Another option is to call a project meeting and tell everyone 'Looks like we have dodged a bullet. The contractor has identified an error in the fire services plans. We can fix it now, and it will only take a month and cost $60,000. If we hadn't have caught this now, it could have cost us 3 months of delay and hundreds of thousands of dollars'.

What do you think happens when you present the information like this? The fire services engineer is motivated to help find a solution (because they will no doubt be aware that they made a mistake). The project team focuses on solving the problem. This both reinforces and builds relationships and trust, which perpetuates a move towards collaboration. It sends the message that 'we solved this problem together' and as a result, the team feel successful. Let's call this the 'good experience'.

Now, the only thing that changed in these two experiences was the 'sense' that you made of the situation. None of the facts changed, but the experience was different. And it was different because you *chose* the narrative of your project. But let me be clear here, I'm not talking about being a spin doctor or polishing a turd. I'm talking about using the facts to frame the experience. Don't play with the facts—that's just lying—instead take the time to see how the facts can be framed to create the experience that you want the team to have.

As I have explained throughout this book, one of your tasks as a project manager is to create confidence for those involved in the project. You can help achieve this by becoming a 'sense-maker'. When things don't go as planned or when unexpected challenges arise, you need to interpret this information. If you don't interpret it, then others will interpret it for you—and you may not like the resulting experience.

The heart of sense-making is being able to understand what is happening and why it is happening and to interpret the information so that a positive experience is created.

As Immanuel Kant explained, if anything has meaning in our lives, it is because we *decided* that thing was important to us. We interpreted information, invented a purpose and then gave that purpose some importance and meaning [21]. This is not a criticism, it is one of the consequences of self-awareness [12]. We all get to choose whether the information we filter into our minds will have meaning for us. It's like gold. Gold was just a rock until someone decided it was valuable. Understanding that we make sense of experiences in order to decide how to feel about value agnostic information, helps us arrive at the project-level, sense-making rule: *Take charge of the narrative to create the best experience.*

Optioneering

Projects evolve. They are delivered in dynamic environments that can create unforeseen challenges. Because of this, it is a fallacy to think that there is a single, best way to get the project where it needs to go. The truth is all projects are equifinal. They can take many paths to achieve the required outcomes [15–17]. Optioneering is a process that allows you to navigate these paths without letting your project run completely rampant. Optioneering creates flexibility while simultaneously ensuring the project process and outcome stays within set parameters.

I like to think of projects as the ultimate 'choose your own adventure' tour. Every tour has its own unique rewards, obstacles and pitfalls, and it's the project manager's job to act as the tour guide. When the project 'tour group' sets off, everyone agrees on the destination, but they don't have the slightest idea which path will lead them where they want to go. However, the tour guide already knows that there is any number of different trails that can be taken to get to the destination, but they don't start by asking the group to make every decision about the paths they want to take. Instead, the guide just gathers the group, gets them moving and then gives them options along the way. 'Would you like to go along the ridge? It has good views but a difficult climb. Or would you prefer to take the valley? It's an easier walk, but you won't get to the same view'. In other words, the guide creates the best experience for the group, based on their combined abilities, by providing them with options that meet their needs at the time but still allows the group to achieve their agreed goal. Essentially, this is optioneering [10].

Optioneering overcomes two human quirks that threaten the value co-creation experience.

Humans are complex and sometimes paradoxical creatures who tend to make decisions based on emotion, and they justify those decisions later with logic. This is never more obvious than when we are faced with a difficult situation and told there is only one solution. Instinctively, we will push back against that solution, even if it is perfectly logical, legitimate and reasonable. Why? Because when we have no choice, we feel powerless and we all hate feeling powerless. So, we instinctively want to reject a perfectly good solution for no other reason other than we don't like how it makes us feel. Then we will justify rejecting that solution by telling ourselves that we want to explore other options first.

'Ah-ha,' I hear you say, 'That's easily fixed. If people feel powerless when they only have one option, then I'll give them as many options as possible to choose from so they can feel in control'.

Nope, sorry. That doesn't work either, because, paradoxically, when people are presented with too many options, they feel powerless as well.

When we are presented with too many solutions to a problem, we assume that a 'best option' must be in there somewhere. This assumption causes us to expend inordinate amounts of time and effort trying to decide between insignificant variables so we can find the 'best option'. When faced with too many options or solutions, humans tend towards analysis paralysis. We get overwhelmed with all the details and just end up having a brain fart. It has been proven that presenting people with too many options can induce a quasi-catatonic state that makes it impossible for them to make decisions [23]. So, once again, we feel powerless because we can't assess all the variables in all the options. This causes us to feel overwhelmed and panicky.

To overcome this tendency towards bipolar powerlessness, you need to decide what options should be considered at what points in your project. To do this, you need to select some workable options from the gamut of possibilities and present these to the project decision-makers. I usually like to present three to five options to choose from. I also make sure I outline the impacts of those options (i.e. make sense), and then I ask the decision-makers how they would like to progress. If you do this well, it won't matter which option the decision-makers select, because you've already stacked the deck. Optioneering allows you to get buy-in from stakeholders while still guiding the outcome so that the project doesn't skew off in the wrong direction.

Optioneering is closely aligned with the ideas of expectation management and sense-making and is the epitome of balancing order and chaos within the project. It is both an art and a science. The art lies in carefully crafting meaningful decisions that create freedom of choice (option-) and the science lies in ensuring that all the options presented can be managed to through to achieve the project's ultimate goal (-eering). This gives us the optioneering project-level, order-generating rule: *Balance freedom and control to create a valuable experience.*

Problem-Solving

Back in 'Project-Level Provisioning Rules', I explained, that projects are just problems that need to be solved. The problem is that this problem has other problems, and by solving some of those problems, you can create new problems. This, of course, becomes a problem. So, you find yourself faced with new problems on almost a daily basis. Until one day, almost magically, all the problems are solved, which, of course, solves the original problem. Project management is as simple as that—No problem!

Understanding that projects are all about solving problems, in many ways, simplifies our role. Rather than getting upset or aggravated when we run into a new problem, all we need to do is understand that by solving each new problem, we are edging closer to our final goal. We don't need to panic when new problems arise because, handled well, each new problem provides an opportunity for value co-creation and a chance to move closer to the completion of our project. So, at this level, the order-generating rule is all about making sure that you are handling the problems well.

Project Management Design Thinking

If you've been a project manager for any length of time, you will have faced your fair share of problems. Some of these are simple and can be solved using the traditional problem-solving model. The traditional problem-solving model has five steps: (1) define the problem, (2) identify alternative solutions, (3) evaluate alternative solutions, (4) select the best solution and (5) implement the best solution. The whole process is clear, simple and intuitive, and each step naturally progresses to the next one (see Fig. 3.7).

Now, this all sounds great. Who doesn't love a nice, linear, easy-to-follow process? When you do come across a problem that can be solved using this model, thank whichever gods you believe in, because you are living a blissful existence. But be careful. Other problems are lurking out there in dark corners, and these problems are not nice, or simple, or easy to solve—these other problems are just downright wicked.

No, I'm not being metaphorical, although I will admit to being overly dramatic. There are problems out there that are defined as wicked problems. A wicked problem is a problem that is difficult or impossible to solve because (a) there is incomplete or contradictory information regarding the problem or its cause; (b) people

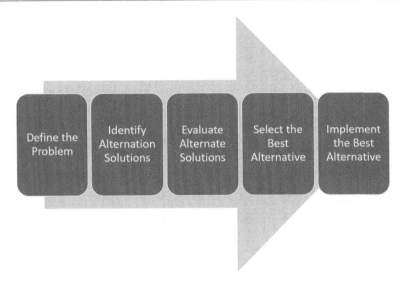

Fig. 3.7 The traditional problem-solving process

cannot agree on exactly what the problem is, or why the problem exists; (c) the cost to find the solution outweighs the financial impacts created by the problem; (d) it is interconnected with other problems which are not readily understood or difficult to solve; or (e) any combination of items (a)–(d).

Now I know what you're thinking. 'I'll stay away from those they don't sound like any fun at all'.

Unfortunately, most projects are or have the potential to include wicked problems. What's worse, you can't solve a wicked problem using the traditional problem-solving process because you get stuck at the first gate: defining the problem. There are times during every project where it will be either extremely difficult or maybe even impossible to clearly define exactly what the problem is. Sure, you can see the impacts of that problem. You can see that it's driving your costs up, slowing your project down or otherwise wreaking havoc on your perfectly good project plan. But just because you can see the impact of the problem doesn't mean you can clearly define what the problem is. Now if you can't clearly define the problem, you can't trace the root cause, and if you can't trace the root cause, how can you possibly decide what the best solution is? In this situation, the traditional problem-solving process is useless. You can't even get to the first gate, let alone find the best solution.

'So, what should a project manager do in these trying times?' I hear you ask. The answer, dear reader, is simple. You use design thinking.

Design thinking is an integrative approach to complex problem-solving that utilises appositional thinking, and abductive reasoning [24, 25].

Design thinking is a collaborative problem-solving process. It leverages multiple sources of knowledge to understand, identify and define a problem while simultaneously developing and testing potential solutions until a suitable solution is created [26, 27]. Rather than a nice, clean, linear process, the strength of the design thinking is its iterative and emergent process. In the design thinking process, developing and testing potential solutions helps inform everyone's understanding of what the problem is. This, in turn, helps refine the potential solutions. These solutions are tested through prototyping until a final solution is agreed upon. This solution can then be clearly outlined and implemented.

The design thinking process can be thought of as a funnel (Fig. 3.8). This funnel has three gateways. Unlike the traditional problem-solving model, the design thinking model starts with the process of simply gathering everything we know about the problem, its impacts and possible causes. In this first stage of the process, you need to draw on as many 'minds' as possible. At this point, you are not trying to identify or define the problem; you are simply seeking to understand as much as possible about what is happening. This first stage can be a bit daunting because you feel like you have huge amounts of data, but no clue what it all means. Don't be alarmed; everyone feels this way. This sense of 'not having a clue about what's going on' is the reason why the first stage in the design thinking funnel is called the *mystery* stage.

As you gather and share more information about the problem, its impacts and potential reasons why it exists, your team will begin to see patterns. You will need multiple perspectives for these patterns to be identified because different team members will view the problem from different vantage points, but together the team will begin to join some of the dots. During this part of the funnel, you need to be both an active participant and a facilitator: a participant to look for the patterns and connections and a facilitator to make sure everyone is getting any new information that is coming in and pushing them to think creatively about the patterns they see. This second stage of the design thinking funnel is called the *heuristic* stage. In the heuristic process, everyone's efforts are focussed on finding a *workable* solution to a difficult problem, not the *best* solution, a *workable* one. During the heuristics stage, you need to answer the question 'Will this work?' not 'Is this the absolute best solution available?' You find the answer through a process of testing and

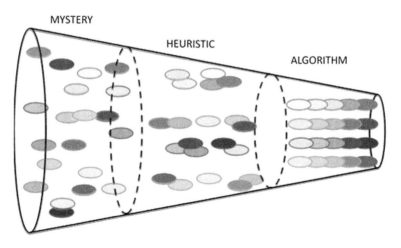

Fig. 3.8 The design thinking funnel [10]

prototyping. For project managers, this process can be as simple as replanning the schedule to see if all the tasks fit together, or it could be as complex as actually building a prototype (e.g. building a temporary sales unit).

The final stage in the design thinking funnel is creating the algorithms for the solution. An algorithm is simply a well-defined and clearly communicated set of implementable steps. In the *algorithm* stage, you need to outline exactly what you want everyone to do to solve the problem. The purpose of the algorithms is to ensure that anyone, with the right technical capability, who is provided with the algorithm, can implement the solution regardless of whether they were involved in the resolution process or not [27–30]. For us, these algorithms can take the form of amended documents and plans, written instructions and specifications—basically anything that we use to tell people how we want the problem resolved.

Using the design thinking funnel to resolve project problems provides a great framework for value co-creation. It demands multiple perspectives and input. It uses the *collective brain* to create and test potential solutions, and it focuses the team on working collaboratively to solve common challenges. Handled well, a wicked problem can be your best friend.

This revelation leads us to our problem-solving project-level, order-generating rule: *Embrace problems as a tool for value co-creation.*

Consensus Building

Not every problem will have a solution that makes everyone rapturously happy. Many of the problems that we face involve conflict: conflict between sponsors and user groups, conflicts between designers and contractors and conflicts between one person's expectations of the project outcome and another's. Our role involves so much potential for interpersonal conflict, that I would argue, if you show me a project manager that has never had to resolve a conflict, then I will show you someone who isn't managing a project.

Now we've already discussed that conflict doesn't always have to involve pistols at ten paces. Most of the conflicts that I have had to resolve come down to people's expectations vs. the finite amount of money that is available to complete the job. What's more, this tension is not always a result of stakeholders or users having champagne tastes and a beer budget. Sometimes these conflicts involve project requirements that are an absolute necessity for one user group, but their needs happen to run contrary to another user group's absolute needs. At times like this, the solution is not as simple as '…cutting the baby in half…' (1 Kings 3:25, NIV). We need a framework for resolving conflicts without compromising the integrity of the project or its outcomes. That framework is consensus building.

Consensus building is a specific form of conflict resolution that combines collaborative problem-solving with value co-creation. It is particularly useful for complex problems that impact multiple, interdependent stakeholders, all of whom have a vested interest in the outcome, but who are not necessarily a cohesive group in terms of the outcomes they want achieved—you know, like a project.

Building consensus is not a 'win-win' philosophy. Sometimes it's an agreement that everyone loses something. I often tell my project managers who are working their way through a consensus-building process, that 'if none of the parties are happy with the result, then you probably arrived at the right solution'.

So, if this consensus building is not about making everyone happy, what is it about?

Fundamentally it's about arriving at the *right* solution. It's about developing a solution that is mutually acceptable to all the parties involved. This is not as easy as it sounds, in fact achieving this will often require all the political skill and emotional intelligence you can muster. Building consensus is not a matter of you making a decision and imposing that on the group. It's not even a matter of you deciding which solution the group should pick. It's about you, as the project manager, guiding a group of invested individuals through a range of difficult choices, until everyone agrees on the right way forward. To do this, you need to take them, step by step, through the consensus-building process.

The first, and perhaps most important, step of this process is making sure the right people are involved. To do this, you need to make sure that you clearly understand what the problem is, who it impacts and how it impacts them. Building consensus requires you to *recruit* the right people into the resolution process so they create value and not just invent roadblocks. Recruiting the right people means finding a balance between people who are passionate about the project, who deeply understand their processes, who are creative and who are solution-focussed. In other words, they need to be willing and able to engage in a collaborative problem-solving process.

Now, let's say that you have managed to recruit a group with the right stuff. This doesn't mean that they are all on the same page in terms of what needs to be done. Several assumptions can choke the life out of a consensus-building process before it even gets started. For instance, don't assume that just because everyone understands what the project is, that they agree on what the project should achieve. Don't assume that just because teams are part of the same organisation that they know what's important to that organisation. Don't assume that because these people have worked side by side for years that they know what each other does or why it needs to be done. And the list goes on. In fact, the only thing you should assume is that *no one is on the same page until you've read them into it.*

Understanding this is the key to consensus building. To build consensus, you need to create group ownership of the problem. If everyone believes that a problem is someone else's to fix, they will not be inclined to engage in finding a solution or be willing to compromise on what they want from the project. It's up to you to make them see and understand how this problem is interconnected with what they want from the project. As soon as people see how the problem will impact them, you will have their attention and they will want to engage.

So, the next step in the process is to make *the* problem—*their* problem.

You do this by letting them get involved. Bring them down into the 'stickiness' that interconnected problems create. Don't try to fix complicated and complex problems behind a veil of secrecy. That will only end in grief. Regardless of whether you came up with a brilliant, logical and elegant solution to a complex challenge, if you have arrived at a solution that impacts others without giving them a chance to be involved in finding a solution that works for them, then you will immediately lose the trust of everyone who feels they got shafted.

The real power of the consensus-building process comes from leveraging the collective power of the group to arrive at an outcome that everyone agrees on—and that's the key statement, 'everyone agrees'. They might not like what happened, but they understand why it happened. They might not be particularly happy with the result, but they agree that it must be done. They might not get exactly what they want, but they completely understand how the solution was developed.

By allowing those who will be impacted by the issue to assist in finding a mutually acceptable solution, you create a powerful value co-creation experience. By allowing them to see the challenge, complexity and interconnectedness of the problem, and then guiding them towards a mutually acceptable solution, you increase the positive experience associated with the project itself.

Human beings love the sense of euphoria that comes with overcoming challenges. The greater the challenge, the better we feel about overcoming it. The same is true in the consensus-building process. Don't be afraid to lead the team into the midst of these complex challenges, to facilitate robust discussions around what can be compromised on for the greater good and to guide them through a collaborative solution-focused process. Just so long as you don't leave them stuck in the problem, you will find that they grow to trust you more for having taken them through the experience.

So our consensus-building project-level, order-generating rule is this: *Achieving the right solution together is better than achieving the best solution alone.*

Summary

In terms of the project-level supporting rules, your role is to manage the multitude of expectations brought into the project, make sense of what is happening, guide the project team using optioneering, solve all the problems that impact the progress of the project and build consensus. The project-level supporting rules are outlined in Table 3.3.

Table 3.3 Project-level supporting rules

Supporting	Requirement	Project-level rule
	Expectation management	Expectations are flexible, bend them.
	Sense-making	Interpret information to create the best experience.
	Optioneering	Balance freedom and control to create a valuable experience.
	Problem-solving	Embrace problems as a tool for value co-creation.
	Consensus building	Achieving the right solution together is better than achieving the best solution alone.

Project-Level Culturalising Rules

Throughout this book, I've used a lot of metaphors—tour groups, tribes and networks. All these metaphors have one thing in common. They all describe groups of people. People are the one thing that all projects have in common. No matter what project you are delivering, it exists because someone, somewhere, needs it. Understanding this leads to one inevitable conclusion: managing people is an important part of the project manager's role.

At the project level, the culturalising rules are all focussed on providing people with meaningful and valuable experiences. But please don't confuse meaningful and valuable for easy and carefree. Projects are difficult. If they weren't difficult, anyone could deliver them, and if anyone could deliver them, then our profession wouldn't need to exist. So, the project-level culturalising rules are about guiding people through an experience that is both trying and difficult in such a way that everyone not only makes it to the end but feels as though all the challenges they faced along the way were worthwhile.

I know what you are thinking, 'That sounds like fun! Sign me up!'

Well, okay then tiger, let's have a look at each of these project-level culturalising rules.

Leadership

I believe leadership is essential in project management. But what is leadership? For that matter, what is management? Is there a difference? If you are struggling to make a clear delineation between the two, don't feel too bad. This question has plagued business thinkers and writers for decades. Countless numbers of books, articles and papers have been written trying to explain the difference.

Everyone seems to have a different idea, and I guess that's understandable. If you are trying to promote your new book on management or leadership, you need to have a new perspective on the idea or no one will buy your book. However, the downside is that people keep creating some new insight, just so they have a unique marketing idea for their latest book (*...and yes, I'm aware of the irony of that last comment while you are reading my book with a new perspective of project management. But hey, too late, you've already bought the book*).

When I was a young buck, I used to read every new book on leadership that I could get my hands on. Some of them were good, others were ho-hum, and, still, others were straight out batshit crazy. However, somewhere along the way, I came across a simple definition that stuck with me: ***you manage tasks, but you lead people***.

Finding this simple explanation was a real eye-opener for me. It suddenly dawned on me that we need to do both, simultaneously, if we are going to successfully deliver our projects. Our role demands that there is a balance between managing tasks and leading people.

Now, I'm sure you were already completely aware of this. But the moment of enlightenment led me to ask another question, 'If we need this balance to deliver our projects, why is most project management literatures focussed primarily on managing tasks?'

Well, I think it's because managing tasks is the easy side of the equation. It's a lot easier to outline the methodologies and processes for planning, controlling and monitoring time, cost and scope than it is to explain the *people* side of what we do.

As a result, the idea of leadership has languished in the dark corners of project management literature like some grotesquely ugly cousin. But, in my opinion, understanding that we have both the opportunity and obligation to lead people through the project experience is critical to fulfilling our role.

Projects involve taking a group of people who might never have worked together before and leading them through a uniquely challenging experience, to achieve an outcome that has never been done before. You simply cannot do that unless you can lead. Because of this, it is my conviction that every project manager needs to be a leader or their project is doomed to failure.

Now, when I say every project manager needs to lead, I'm not talking about whether you are the boss or not. I'm not talking about the title on your business card. I'm talking about the type of leadership that doesn't need a title to be recognised. It's the unshakable belief that being a project manager is both a privilege and a responsibility. It's understanding that when someone makes you their project manager, they are handing you control of their money, their time and their goals so that you can help them achieve something they can't.

This brings with it an obligation to make sure that you are not just meandering aimlessly through the project delivery process. Accepting the role of project manager demands that you also accept responsibility and accountability for navigating through all the unique challenges that will be faced. To do that means actively taking the reins and where necessary driving the project forward.

The Australian Defence Force has a simple maxim which they drill into all their new officers to help them understand the importance of leading; it goes like this, 'if you are put in charge, then be in charge'. This simple, yet powerful statement captures the essence of our first project-level, culturalising rule: *If you have been given a project, then lead the project.*

Team Building

Have you ever seen the EDS advertisement of cowboys herding cats? If not, do yourself a favour and have a look (https://www.youtube.com/watch?v=Pk7yqlTMvp8). As a project manager, you will find it very funny and yet, at the same time, very difficult to watch.

It's funny because every project manager can relate to it. I am yet to meet a project manager who doesn't immediately understand the expression 'herding the cats'. We have all experienced the joys of trying to get everyone focussed on the same thing at the same time so we can all arrive at the destination together. But this advertisement is also difficult for project managers to watch for all the same reasons. We know exactly how hard it can be to lead the people, manage the tasks, meet the project criteria and do it all within the constraints of time, cost and quality that have been imposed on us. As hard as this is, it is made even more difficult when we try to achieve this with a group of individuals rather than a cohesive team.

Achieving your project objectives requires more than simply having a group of people with the right technical and professional skills working on the project. It takes a team, and teams don't just spontaneously develop. Someone has to build them.

There are a number of ways that you can build a team. Who knows, there could be as many ways to build a team as there are projects to deliver. Despite the myriad of different ways to build the team, there are also common elements that must be in place if you are going to forge a group into a team. There are five non-negotiable elements to building a team, and if you fail to put any of these in place, your team-building efforts will fail [31].

First and foremost, in all your dealings with team members, you must always demonstrate respect and consideration. Nothing will destroy a team faster than demeaning team member's efforts and ideas. Word gets around quickly. If you start disrespecting any of the team, the rest will soon get the message. One of the best pieces of advice I ever got concerning this was to make sure you enter every single team engagement using the MRI—the most respectful interpretation [32]. In other words, when a team member disagrees with you, challenges an idea or offers an 'out-of-the-box' solution, always respond by making the most respectful interpretation possible of their reasons for doing so. Even if you eventually decide not to take their idea on board, they, and the rest of the team, will see how you behaved and know that you respect both them and their contribution.

The second element is to clearly identify job responsibilities and performance expectations. Whether this is a clear charter of roles and responsibilities or a clear set of action items following a meeting, people need to know what's required of them to function at their best. Ironically, over the years, the one team member I have seen that is most likely to cross lines of responsibility and interfere with other's roles is the project manager. Yes, we have a key role to play in connecting all the team members together, but we are not the sponsors, users, designers or contractors. Part of building a strong team is demonstrating trust in people's ability to achieve that part of the project that they were brought in to do. So, stay in your lane. Direct, guide, facilitate and coordinate their activities, but don't do their job for them.

The third element is clear communication. This means making sure that everyone is clear about what is happening and why. It's about ensuring consistent messaging between the team as a whole and all the individuals in that team. This can often be more difficult than it sounds in a complex and dynamic environment. Sometimes we have to make important decision quickly. When these decision impact others, we need to inform them quickly so that their time is not being wasted. It's a mark of respect. We also need to make sure that we are regularly recalibrating all the activities of the team, to make sure everyone is keeping up with the changing landscape.

The fourth element is rewarding team-building efforts. To build a team, you have to think in terms of the team. This means finding ways to reward as a 'unit' not as individuals. Having team goals is only the start; to close the loop, you need to reward the team, as a team, for achieving these goals. One way to do this is through 'milestone parties'. These can be as simple as a few rounds of drinks and a pizza or as extravagant as taking the project team and their life partners away for a holiday. It depends completely on the size of the project and the size of the milestone that has been reached. What you do is not the important part—it's doing it as a team that's important.

The fifth and final element necessary for successful team building is to encourage loyalty to the team. Encouraging team loyalty is not about having a few parlour tricks up your sleeve to fool people into being loyal. Building team loyalty starts with you—your attitude and your ethos. You have to believe, in your heart of hearts, that investing the time and effort into building a team is better than spending that time managing a group of professional 'cats'. If you truly believe this, then the actions needed to build the team will come naturally to you—things like being ready to jump in and help during times of high pressure or tight time frames or reacting quickly to the needs of a team member and even using the terms 'us', 'we' and 'the team' rather than 'you', 'they' or 'I'. All of these actions send clear messages. We are a team. We face common challenges. We have a common goal, and we need to reach it together.

The networks that are drawn to the project will provide you with a pool of talented professionals. You will be handed a group of highly trained, highly skilled, multidisciplinary professionals—but that's not a project team. It's a group, and this leads us to our team building project-level culturalising rule: *If you want a project team, you must build it yourself.*

Storytelling

Human beings learn through experiences. Sometimes these experiences are ours, and sometimes they are other peoples. We learn from other people's experiences by listening to the stories they tell. Gregory Berry tells us that '…stories are the fundamental way through which we understand our world…' (p. 59) [33]. Some philosophers have argued that the concept of self-awareness is simply the ability to know how your story fits within the greater story of history.

Stories are powerful because they connect with us on an emotional level. There is something about a good story that causes us to suspend our rational thinking and let the message of the story sink right into our souls [34]. Stories can entertain and teach us, they can delight and extol us, or they can frighten or inspire us. Harris and Barnes [35] have described stories as the most basic tools of leadership.

But why are stories so powerful? Well primarily because they can reach across boundaries of culture, education or age. Stories bring knowledge to life by helping us put information into coherent patterns for easy recall. They can make history contemporary by building bridges from the past to explain the present. They link the present to the future by reminding us that, although our current circumstances might be unknown and frightening, others have been through unknown and frightening places before and lived to tell the story.

Stories allow us to transfer tacit knowledge contextually. When you tell a story, you can provide nuances that simply can't be related in codified routines and rules. Boal and Schultz [36] argue that '...routines and rules appear [to newcomers] as disembodied imprints of history, they are not sufficient for understanding and knowledge creation...' (p. 419). Rules, routines and regulations create efficiency but they don't encourage innovation and creativity. You can use rules, routines and regulations to manage a project, but not to lead one. Although rules and routines create effective management, don't forget that they also have their own stories. If you know the story, then you have a true understanding of why that rule, routine or regulation is needed and perhaps, more importantly, when it should be bent, broken or even ignored.

But stories are more than containers for knowledge. Since the dawn of time, stories, or oral history, have been central to the idea of belonging. All cultures, societies, nations and teams have their own stories. You can tell the group's story to someone who is not part of the group but it won't have the same meaning that it will for *insiders*. These stories become the passport for being considered 'one of us'. If an individual wants to belong, they must both know and accept the stories. Knowing and accepting these stories is important because hidden within them are the basic principles of how members of this group live, think and behave. Stories are the living memories of the group and the foundation of the group's culture. When group members can exchange these stories with one another, they become part of the collective. More importantly, if someone can re-tell the group's stories, then the story moves from being a story that belongs to *that group* and becomes *their story*.

So, it is imperative at the project level that you create and tell stories. There are as many different stories to tell as there are experiences and events in your life. I can't tell you what stories to tell, but I can give some advice that will help you tell your stories. Here are some simple basic rules for project storytelling.

1. Make sure the story has a clear message. Don't ramble or send mixed messages.
2. Make sure the story is relevant to the situation you are in.
3. Don't tell stories that are self-serving or boastful.
4. Don't 'preach'.
5. Stay away from sarcastic stories.
6. If possible, include some playful or self-deprecating humour. Seeing the funny side of your failures creates trust with the listener.

In their research about leadership storytelling, Boal and Schultz [36] found that effective leaders tell four types of stories. Firstly, they tell stories that link events together in the chronological order so everyone can follow the progression of certain decisions. These stories create *temporal coherence*. The second type of story creates *cultural coherence*. A leader uses these stories to recount the specific events that helped develop the group's culture and how that culture has helped the group get through difficult times. The third type of story highlights a unifying or recurrent idea. This type of story creates *thematic coherence*, and leaders use them to help the group make sense of events by showing them a common thread amongst the events. The fourth and final type of story is one that links cause and effect. The leader uses this type of story to create *causal coherence*. They use this story type to explain how the paths taken in the past have created the present options and then how each of those options can create a different future for the group.

Perhaps the most important reason to include storytelling in the project-level culturalising rules is because of the role it plays in value co-creation. We have already looked at how stories create belonging. We have looked at how stories can transition from the *group's* story to *my* story when it gets retold. However, the most important aspect of storytelling is that each person in your team is a co-author of your project's story.

Storytelling is a reciprocal process; both the storyteller and the listener need to actively engage for it to work. When both parties actively engage in the process, the story comes to life. Not only does the story impart a message, but it forms a special bond between the parties involved—they have connected on an emotional level. What's more, when the listener re-tells the story, it becomes part of them, because now it's 'their story' to tell. So, as a story is told and retold, it moves from being entertainment to becoming myth and legend. Long after the original storyteller has moved on, the story continues to jump from re-teller to listener, reinforcing the core messages, connecting people on an emotional level and, most importantly, converting 'outsiders' to 'insiders'. This is why storytelling is so important for project managers. *Converting project experiences and events into our story* is essential for the development of a team's culture, and that's why it becomes one of our project-level, culturalising rules.

Summary

In terms of these project-level culturalising rules, our role as project managers is to take different people, from different walks of like, who have different goals, skills and understanding, and mould them into an effective team which can deliver the unique outcomes of the project. We do this by demonstrating leadership, building our team and telling stories. The project-level culturalising rules are outlined in Table 3.4.

Table 3.4 Project-level culturalising rules

Culturalising	Requirement	Project-level rule
	Leadership	If you have been given a project, then lead the project
	Team building	To have a team, you must build a team
	Storytelling	Convert project experiences and events into 'our' story

References

1. van der Hoorn B (2015) Playing projects: identifying flow in the 'lived experience'. Int J Proj Manag 33(5):1008–1021
2. Broadwell MM (1969) Teaching for learning (XVI). Gospel Guardian 20(41):1–3
3. Chew WC (2012) Quantum mechanics made simple: lecture notes. http://wcchew.ece.illinois.edu/chew/course/QMALL20121005.pdf
4. Dirac PAM (1981) The principles of quantum mechanics (no. 27). Oxford University Press
5. Nana L, John G, Ivette F, Vlatko V, Kavan M, David Edward B (2016) Quantum thermodynamics for a model of an expanding Universe. Class Quantum Gravity 33(3):035003
6. Pestana MS (2001) Complexity theory, quantum mechanics and radically free self determination. J Mind Behav 22(4):364–388
7. E. M. Goldratt, Theory of constraints. North River Croton-on-Hudson, 1990
8. Izmailov A, Korneva D, Kozhemiakin A (2016) Effective project management with theory of constraints. Procedia Soc Behav Sci 229:96–103
9. Goldratt EM (1997) Critical chain. 1997. Virine, Lev and Trumper, Michael. Schedule Network Analysis Using Event Chain. sl: ProjectDecisions.org
10. Usher GS (2019) Creating confidence amongst complexity: the 'lived experience' of client-side project managers in the Australian Construction Sector. Ph.D., Business and Management, University of Southern Queensland, Brisbane, Australia
11. Usher GS (2019) Next decision node (NDN) planning: an ambidextrous planning model. Int J Manag Proj Bus
12. Beaman AL, Klentz B, Diener E, Svanum S (1979) Self-awareness and transgression in children: two field studies. J Pers Soc Psychol 37(10):1835
13. Drucker PF (1955) The practice of management. Butterworth Heinemann, Oxford
14. Söderholm A (2008) Project management of unexpected events. Int J Proj Manag 26(1):80–86
15. Usher G, Whitty SJ (2017) Identifying and managing drift-changes. Int J Proj Manag 35(4):586–603
16. Usher G, Whitty SJ (2017) Project Management Yinyang: coupling project success and client satisfaction. Proj Manage Res Pract 4
17. Usher G, Whitty SJ (2017) The final state convergence model. Int J Manag Proj Bus 10(4):770–795
18. Hoffman T (2007) Great expectations. Computerworld 41(23):38–38
19. Laufer A, Hoffman EJ, Russell JS, Cameron WS (2015) What successful project managers do. MIT Sloan Manag Rev 56(3):43
20. Manson M (2016) The subtle art of not giving a fuck. Pan Macmillian, Sydney, Australia
21. Kant I (1963) What is enlightenment? On history. Bobbs-Merril, Indianapolis, pp 3–10
22. Kant I (1998) Critique of pure reason. Cambridge University Press
23. Mann D (2002) Analysis paralysis: when root cause analysis isn't the way. TRIZ J
24. Ben Mahmoud-Jouini S, Midler C, Silberzahn P (2016) Contributions of design thinking to project management in an innovation context. Proj Manag J 47(2):144–156
25. Brown T (2008) Design thinking. Harv Bus Rev 86(6):84–92
26. Gloppen J (2009) Perspectives on design leadership and design thinking and how they relate to European service industries. Des Manag J 4(1):33–47
27. Boland RJ, Collopy F (2004) Managing as Designing. Stanford University Press, California
28. Martin R (2010) Design thinking: achieving insights via the "knowledge funnel". Strateg Leadersh 38(2):37–41
29. Martin RL (2009) The design of business why design thinking is the next competitive advantage. Harvard Business Press, Boston, MA. http://ezproxy.usq.edu.au/login?url=http://library.books24x7.com/library.asp?^B&bookid=36319
30. Usher GS, Whitty SJ (2018) The client-side project manager: a practitioner of design. Proj Manage Res Pract 5:6147

31. Tippett DD, Peters JF (1995) Team building and project management: how are we doing? Project Management Institute
32. Jans N (2018) Leadership secrets of the Australian Army: learn from the best and inspire your team for great results. Allen & Unwin
33. Berry GR (2001) Telling stories: making sense of the environmental behaviour of chemical firms. J Manag Inq 10:58–73
34. Mládková L (ed) (2014) Storytelling and leadership skills of managers, vol 2. Academic Conferences International Limited, Kidmore End, pp 667–675
35. Harris J, Kim Barnes B (2006) Leadership storytelling. Ind Commer Train 38(7):350–353
36. Boal KB, Schultz PL (2007) Storytelling, time, and evolution: the role of strategic leadership in complex adaptive systems. Leadersh Q 18(4):411–428

The Experience

4

Understanding the Experience

Now that we have discussed the elephant and the eco-system, it's time to move onto what I believe could be the most important aspect of project management—*the experience.*

In 2006, the Rethinking Project Management Network published a two-year study which investigated the future challenges of our profession. One of the areas explored was the need to shift our focus from 'project creation' to 'value creation' [1]. However, to achieve this, the researchers argued that we will need to reconceptualise project management as a social process, not a technical one [2]. Facilitating this change will require us to expand our current myopic focus on project management 'hard skills' and develop more 'soft skills'. This call to move to a more human-focussed version of project management is not something we can just ignore. Many world-renowned project management researchers believe the survival of our profession will be determined by our ability to develop a better understanding of the experience of project management instead of our historical, singular focus on the mechanics of project delivery [2].

I agree 100% with these researchers. It is my firm belief that, as project managers, we have a critical role to play in choreographing the project experience so everyone involved can co-create value. Unfortunately, because value is subjective, there isn't an algorithm or standardised process to do this. The only way you can really do it is to understand how value is created in projects so you can begin to work your magic.

For me, the process of understanding value co-creation through my projects began when I was faced with two paradoxical project outcomes. One was a disappointing success and the other a delightful failure. To start drilling into the process

© The Author(s), under exclusive license to Springer Nature Switzerland AG 2021
G. Usher, *Project Management in the 21st Century*, Management
for Professionals, https://doi.org/10.1007/978-3-030-71543-4_4

of co-creating value, let's look at these two projects: what happened, why it happened, and what that means for us moving forward.

The Case of the Disappointing Success

The goal of this project was to deliver training facilities for a government organisation. This organisation intended to use these facilities to train seven different user groups, each of whom had quite different training needs.

When my firm was engaged, the sponsor confirmed they had $8 million set aside for the project. I reviewed the cost plans and was satisfied that the finances provisioned for the project were sufficient for the planned works. The sponsor also advised that the project had to be completed in 18 months. Together we decided that a design and construct methodology was the best fit for the organisation's risk profile, budget and time constraint.

My project team spent the first few weeks engaging with the different user groups and getting into the detail of what the training facilities needed to do and how it needed to be done. From this, we were able to develop the design brief and tender documents. We procured the contractor and began the detailed design process. In the final month of the design process, the sponsor's rep was diagnosed with a medical condition and had to step down from his role. A new sponsor's rep was appointed.

And that's when the fun started.

We had just started pouring the second stage of the foundations when the global financial crisis hit. The sponsor decided to continue with the project, but they had to cut the budget back to $5.4 million (*so much for my detailed review of the initial business plans, but hey this is why I love project work.*)

We had to move quickly because the contractor was spending money by the day on the construction. Armed with the new budget, I called together the sponsor and user group reps, the project team, the design team and the contractor and facilitated a scope reduction workshop. Through this, we established a new, reduced project scope and created a prioritised list of scope items that could be reintroduced into the project as risks were retired and contingency funds were released.

The rest of the construction took about 9 months to complete. Throughout this process, I met regularly with the sponsor and user reps, as well as the project and construction teams, to make sure everyone was up to date with our progress. As the works progressed and risk contingencies were retired, we were able to reintroduce several previously removed scope items from the endorsed scope list.

Two weeks before practical completion, the original sponsor's rep returned. He came back from his medical leave and resumed his role (in a somewhat honorary capacity). While he was away, he had not been kept in the loop about what had happened regarding the budget cut, the scope reduction, our risk mitigation strategies or the reintroduction of scope items that we thought we had lost in the budget cut.

Practical completion was achieved 2 days ahead of the revised schedule and came in 0.15% under the revised budget. Booyah! We had done it. There was a lot of smiling faces and back-slapping as we reflected on how we had managed to snatch success from the jaws of failure. From the perspective of the traditional project management criteria—time, cost and scope—the project was a success.

Fast forward one month, I went back to the facility to conduct a post-occupancy evaluation. This is a workshop which brings the sponsor, user group reps, designers, contractor and project team back together to review the project and identify any lessons learned. The meeting was going as expected with the sponsor and user group reps commending the project team for completing the project on time and under budget despite some significant challenges. Everyone was all smiles…until the returned sponsor's rep stood up.

The sponsor's rep used this time to express his displeasure at the project. He went on, and on, and on about how disappointed he was. He talked about the scope items that got cut and how they would have made all the difference to the usability of the facilities. He talked about how good the facilities *could have been*, if only we had delivered what we originally set out to do. He finished off his tirade by stating '…I don't know why we didn't just shelf the whole thing when the budget got cut. We've spent $5M on a building that's basically useless…'.

What the hell?

This little ray of sunshine left me feeling confused and gutted. We were on time, under budget and achieved the approved scope. Seriously, didn't this guy understand that the goal of any project is to tick these three boxes. We had managed some extraordinary challenges, overcome massive hurdles and circumvented major obstacles. What's more, we delivered a project, that by all traditional metrics, was a resounding success. This guy should just get the hell of his soapbox, pat me on the back, thank me for my great work and be deliriously satisfied with the outcome. What an amateur!

That is, of course, unless our traditional measures of project success don't necessarily equate to someone's sense of satisfaction.

Hmmm, hold onto that thought for now. We'll come back to it.

The Case of the Delightful Failure

This project was delivered for a not-for-profit service provider in Australia. The goal of this project was to prepare a business case for the development of a major property development. My firm was engaged to undertake scope definition, procure the technical disciplines required to develop some masterplan options and draft a business case for endorsement by the sponsor's governing body.

At the commencement of the project, the sponsor confirmed the project budget ($0.35 million—and yes, I checked it) and outlined the delivery timeframe (12 weeks for business case development and submission—yep, I checked that too).

The governing body that needed to endorse the final business case consisted of five levels of organisational hierarchy and representatives from ten different departments. Many of these people had never been involved in a construction project any bigger than building their own home. These reps had wide-ranging, and sometimes conflicting, expectations regarding the final outcomes of the project. These included differing opinions about what the project's priorities were, what facilities should be included in the development, and disagreements about what funding models to adopt. You know, just some minor things.

My project team engaged with each of the user and governance groups individually to gather and document their expectations concerning the project outcomes. We consolidated all of this into a user requirement matrix and provided it to everyone for review. I then facilitated meetings with all the representatives and gained consensus from the group on each of the project requirements and how important each element was to the overall organisation. This process resulted in a fully documented user requirements brief that outlined and prioritised all the stakeholder's expectations regarding the final project outcomes.

From this, the project team developed four master-planned options for the site. Multiple funding options were explored for each master-planned option, and the associated financial hurdle rates were assessed. When I eventually did get the final business case endorsed, the project had run 18 weeks over the original forecast and come in 40% over budget. From the perspective of the traditional project management criteria—time, cost and scope—the project was a complete failure.

However, when we did the project completion workshop, the organisation's reps and governance team were ecstatic. They gushed about how great the whole process was. They commended the project team for successfully developing the business case, managing the complex stakeholder and governance environment and mentoring the governance team through some significant challenges. Not once did anyone mention the significant budget overrun or my failure to hit the nominated deadline. Instead, they asked me to prepare two more business case for other development sites and engaged my firm to manage almost $0.5 Billion of construction.

Once again, I was confused.

In terms of everything I had been taught about project management success, this project was a complete flop. But here was this group of stakeholders walking around spruiking about what a great project manager I was.

Seriously, what the hell is going on?

To understand how one project can be a disappointing success and the other a delightful failure, you need to come to grips with two phenomena—'systemic discourses' and 'coupling'. So, let's have a look at each of these.

A Brief Introduction to Systemic Discourses and Coupling

What shape is purple?

Well, that's a nonsense question, I can hear you thinking, and I agree. None of us would think of asking this question to a sponsor or user rep. However, this is essentially what we do when using project success as a measure of stakeholder satisfaction. We ask a nonsense question.

The problem stems from a basic misunderstanding of success and satisfaction. For decades, project managers have treated project success and stakeholder satisfaction as synonymous terms. Project completed on time and under budget? Check.

Client satisfied? Check. But the problem is they are not the same thing—not even close. In fact, they are so different, that they exist in completely different systemic discourses.

Systemic what? Systemic discourses. Here, let me explain.

A discourse is a form of communication used to explain or describe an item, event or phenomena. These discourses can be grouped into different systems of communication (i.e. systemic discourses).

Our original question 'What shape is purple?' shows these different systems of communication at work. When we discuss shapes, we use geometric patterns, angles and lengths to communicate our thoughts. For colours, we use shades, tones and hues. Both are perfectly legitimate ways of communicating; however, they operate in different systems. Because of this, although we understand all the words in the question, 'What shape is purple?', there is no way that we can make those terms translate into an answer that makes any sense. This is why Lyotard [3] writes that '...there is no unity in language. There are islands of language, each of them ruled by different regimes, untranslatable into the others...'.

There is a wide range of these different systemic discourses, and we use them every day—mostly without even knowing that we are doing it. However, for our discussion on project management, I want to look at two of these, the scientific system and the emotional system.

Epistemologically, the scientific system is a positivist system. A positivist system assesses information objectively and empirically and uses binary responses (i.e. yes/no; true/false) to determine the validity of information [4]. For example, I might hypothesise that a large rock falls faster than a small rock when dropped out of a window. Using the scientific system, I can test this objectively and empirically through a multitude of experiments, each one designed to have one of two binary outcomes, 'yes' or 'no'. I measure the diameters of each rock and then drop them out of the window and time their fall. Did the larger rock hit before the ground before the smaller rock? Yes/No. I can do this experiment repeatedly, but the answers will only ever be binary—yes or no.

When project managers assess project success, they generally use the scientific discourse. Was the project delivered ahead of the specific deadline? Yes/No. Was it completed under budget? Yes/No. If the answer to the question is 'yes', then that element of the project is classified as a success. If we get enough 'yeses' registered against the critical success factors (*that we created*), then we generally pat ourselves on the back and declare the project a 'success'.

The other system is the emotional system. Epistemologically, this system is an interpretivist system. An interpretivist system assesses information subjectively and intuitively. There is no way to 'test' the validity of the information in this system. It just is. Assessments are based on the feelings that people have about certain information or events, and only the person making the assessment gets to decide how they feel about that information.

When we, as project managers, seek feedback on stakeholder satisfaction, we are using an emotional discourse. Unlike the 'success' question that can be answered with either yes or no, the question of whether a stakeholder is satisfied with the project can fall anywhere on a continuum that ranges from 'completely dissatisfied' to 'completely satisfied'. It is entirely possible to have stakeholders that are 'somewhat satisfied' or 'satisfied with X but not with Y'. What's more, we can't argue with people about how they feel. If someone tells us they are unhappy or dissatisfied with the outcome of our project, there is no test that we can do to prove to them that they are, in fact, 'satisfied' even though they don't feel that way.

So, if project success and stakeholder satisfaction are as different as shapes and colours, why do so many stakeholder's feel satisfied when a project meets one of the success factors?

Well that, dear reader, is a phenomenon known as 'coupling'.

Back when we looked at the eco-system-level supporting rules, I introduced you to the process of decontextualisation and recontextualisation. This same process occurs between systemic discourses. What happens is that key points are decoded from the logic and language of one system, transferred as core ideas and then recoded into another system using the logic and language of that system. The simple term for this process is *coupling*, and the tighter the coupling, the more seamless the information transfer will appear.

Let me give you an example of how quickly and seamlessly coupling can work. Have you ever found that a smell can evoke a memory? Maybe the smell of baking reminds you of your grandmother. Or maybe a fragrance reminds you of a lost love? Now we can all agree that the smell is not the memory, but the coupling between the olfactory sense and the cognitive recall occurs so quickly that we don't ever stop to think about the process. In fact, we probably didn't even notice it taking place.

The same can happen in our projects. In our projects, the coupling can be so tight that objectively assessed *success* becomes confused for subjectively assessed *satisfaction*.

For some of our project team members and stakeholders, this coupling could be so tight that they, themselves, cannot differentiate that two systemic discourses are at work. However, there will be others for whom this coupling is quite loose. For them, the achievement of empirically provable outcomes will not elicit feelings of satisfaction. What's more, some of your project team and stakeholders might be completely non-plussed about the achievement of traditional project success factors altogether and derive their sense of satisfaction from god-knows-where.

In projects, value derives from a complex coupling of both success and satisfaction. Individually, neither of these phenomena are sufficient to guarantee a project experience that everyone considers valuable. To guarantee an experience that a person considers valuable, you achieve both simultaneously.

I wish I could give you a simple way of determining which of your team members or stakeholders have tightly or loosely coupled systemic discourses, but alas, I cannot.

However, not all is lost. At least, you know different discourse systems exist in your projects, and you can understand that they are both constantly at play. What's more, you now understand why it is possible to have disappointing project successes and delightful project failures. And from that understanding, we can begin to explore value co-creation and how you can manage it in your project.

The Value Co-Creation Experience

As we saw at the beginning of this book, the old project management paradigm employs a chain to create value. This value chain makes several assumptions, not the least of which is that value is an inherent attribute of the project we deliver. It is an old way of thinking founded on ideas that are over a century old.

For our profession to thrive in the future, we need to make a fundamental shift in the way we see value in projects. This requires a complete step-change from meeting success criteria to creating value [5]. But to make this shift, we first need to get a better understanding of phenomenological value and how it is created.

Perhaps one most significant concepts that we need to grasp to make this move is to realise that our role is *not to create value* for our project stakeholders, but our role is to *mobilise them to create their own value* from the project experience [6]. In other words, rather than dictate to our stakeholders what value the project will deliver to them, we need to become facilitators who help them find their own personalised value experience through our project.

You might be thinking, 'This sounds a lot more difficult than just knuckling down and delivering a project with the specified scope that is on time and on budget', and you would be right. It is more difficult. It's infinitely more difficult. It requires a set of skills that are not yet taught in project management courses. But just because something is difficult, doesn't mean it can't be mastered.

If anything, we have just identified that there may be a whole set of project management competencies about which you are currently unconsciously incompetent. So, let's elevate that to conscious incompetence and make the pursuit of a new value paradigm your latest personal development project.

The 4C's of Value Co-Creation

As I said earlier, in this new way of thinking, your role as a project manager is to facilitate the co-creation of value *through* your project *for* your stakeholders. To do this, you need to be familiar with the 4C's of value co-creation. These are:

1. Connection.
2. Comprehension.
3. Collaboration.
4. Coupling.

If you don't have the 4C's in place, then your project team and stakeholders can't extract value from their project experience.

Connection

To get value from an experience, we must be connected to it. We need to be aware of the experience (conscious), and we need to be emotionally invested in it. For our project teams and stakeholders to get value from the project experience, they need to feel a connection to the project.

Creating this connection for other people can be challenging, but it's not impossible. There are two simple, but powerful, strategies that you can use to emotionally connect people to your project so they can extract value from the experience. These strategies are 'make them see' and 'make them feel'.

Helping project teams and stakeholders 'see' demands we move past the rational and logical aspects of what we are doing and tap into the emotional aspect of our project. We will never get people to connect with our project by showing them charts, graphs and risk matrices. Sure, we can use these to inform them about the project, but none of this is really connecting **with** the project. To do that, they need to 'see' the project.

Jon Stegnor [7] recounts a great story that illustrates the power of seeing and how this creates connection:

> ...We had a problem with our whole purchasing process.... I thought we had an opportunity to drive down purchasing costs not by 2 per cent but by something in the order of $1 billion over the next five years... This would not be possible, however, unless many people...saw the opportunity, which for the most part they did not. So nothing was happening.
>
> To get a sense of the magnitude of the problem, I asked one of our summer students to do a small study of how much we pay for the different kinds of gloves used in our factories and how many different gloves we buy. I chose one item to keep it simple, something all the plants use and something we can all easily relate to.
>
> When the student completed the project, she reported that our factories were purchasing 424 different kinds of gloves! ...Every factory had its own supplier and their own negotiated price. The same glove could cost $5 at one factory and $17 at another...When I examined what she had found, even I couldn't believe how bad it was.
>
> The student was able to collect a sample of every one of the 424 gloves. She tagged each one with the price on it ...We gathered them all up and put them in our boardroom one day. Then we invited all the division presidents to come to visit the room. What they saw was a large, expensive table, normally clean or with a few papers, now stacked high with gloves. Each of our executives stared at this display for a minute. Then each said something like, "We buy all these different kinds of gloves?" Well, as a matter of fact, yes we do. "Really? "Yes, really. ... They looked at two gloves that seemed exactly alike, yet one was marked $3.22 and the other $10.55.
>
> This demonstration quickly gained notoriety. The gloves became part of a travelling roadshow. They went to every division. They went to dozens of plants. Many, many people had the opportunity to look at the stacks of gloves. The roadshow reinforced at every level of the organization a sense of "this is how bad it is....

This story is a powerful example that, before our project team and stakeholders will connect with the project experience, we need to help them 'see' the project. Most of the time, we won't be able to do something as overt as throw gloves on the boardroom table, so we need to get a bit more creative.

At the start of a project, we must rely heavily on our knowledge bridging, sense-making and storytelling abilities to build a picture in people's minds to help them 'see'. Later, as the project develops, we can employ other techniques and tools like models, prototypes or visualisations. We can take people on-site tours of other projects to show them scale, size and height. How we make them see is irrelevant, just as long as we can take our project out of the PowerPoint presentation, cost spreadsheet and risk matrix and 'show' them what the project actually is.

But just seeing the project is not enough for your team and stakeholders to get value from the project experience. As we have already explored, phenomenological value is subjective. It's created at an emotional level. So, before the project experience can be valuable to anyone, they need to 'feel' something about it.

When I was researching my thesis [8], I spent a lot of time talking with project managers about if and why they liked their job. In over 70 interviews, not one of them said '…I love spreadsheets…'. However, they did say things like '…I love the challenge…', '…I love the thrill of doing what looked impossible…', '…I get a real sense of satisfaction from taking a project from an idea to a building…', 'I love the variety, I never really know what my day holds…'.

How about you? If you enjoy project management, why do you enjoy it?

I'd bet my bottom dollar it's because of the emotional fulfilment you get from doing something challenging, unique and difficult. So, if you feel that way, why do you think your project team or stakeholders would be any different? After all, most of us are like the rest of us.

If you want people to get value from the project experience, you need to let them become emotionally invested in it. Let them experience the highs and lows. Let them feel the challenges of project work. Give them a reason to connect.

As project managers, one of the most powerful tools we have in our emotional arsenal is own feelings about our projects. Research has shown that good project managers have certain key mindsets that make it possible for them to successfully connect people with their projects. Really good project managers are optimistic, ambiguity tolerant, able to take a holistic view of their project and particularly good at integrative thinking [9].

What we need to do to create an emotional connection for others is to 'infect' them with these feelings. We need to be able to say 'Yes, it's hard, but it's not impossible', 'Of course, we don't know everything, but we know enough to start', and 'Yes there are problems, but we are making progress'.

Leading people to connect emotionally with the project experience can be dangerous. Some people are not built to cope with the stuff that we do. That's not their fault, it's just how it is. So, we need to be their guide, their coach and their cheer squad. We need to get them to 'feel' connected. But we also need to make sure they feel safe amid our beautiful, chaotic, crazy project. We are the ones that need to be setting the tone, we must be the exemplar for the emotional connection. In short, we need to become the emotional anchor of the entire project experience. Because until we can make them 'see' and 'feel' the project, they will never be able to get a valuable experience from being involved.

So, the first C of the value co-creation experience is *connection* (Fig. 4.1).

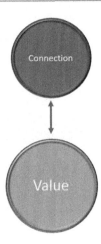

Fig. 4.1 Value co-creation needs connection

Comprehension

The next C in our value quadrat is comprehension. The English word 'comprehension' derives from the Latin word 'comprenedere' meaning 'to grasp'. For someone to get value from an experience, they need to be able to comprehend that experience. Comprehending is completely different from knowing about something or even believing in something. Knowing, believing and comprehending are three distinct states of knowledge [10]. Let me give you an example of how these different knowledge states work.

I grew up and still live in Queensland Australia. In the depths of winter, the temperature outside might get as low as 10 °C. Some years ago, I was invited to present my research at Nankai University in Tianjin, China. My wife and I googled the temperate in China at the time when we were going to be over there and found it could get as low as −10 °C. So, sitting in my nice warm house in Queensland, Australia, I now *knew* that the temperature could be −10 °C. Not only that, but I *believed* that it would be. But neither the knowledge nor the belief meant anything to me. It wasn't until I walked out of the International Airport for the first time that I could comprehend just how cold −10 °C is. For me, the experience of walking out into that temperature literally took my breath away. I had never experienced anything so cold in my life.

When we talk about knowing something, we mean that we are aware of it. There was a point when we were not aware, and there is a point when we are. Before the invitation, I was not even aware there was a city called Tianjin, let along how cold it got in winter. Knowing is awareness.

When we talk about believing something, we mean that we have made a judgement about the truth of that thing. In my China example, I had no reason to think that Google was lying to me, so I accepted what I read as truth, even though I had never been to China nor had any way of testing the veracity of that information. Believing is faith.

However, the reality was that neither knowing nor believing created any value for me. It was just disassociated information that I was aware of and believed in. It *meant* nothing. I had no grid of reference and no framework to comprehend what that information meant. I now had new knowledge, but I didn't and, in fact, couldn't understand what that knowledge meant. It wasn't until I took one step outside the heated airport terminal that I comprehended just how cold −10 °C really is. Comprehending is understanding.

For people to find value in an experience, they need to reach this third level of knowledge. They need to be able to associate the information they have with something that makes sense to them. So, how does all this work in your project?

Let me give you an example from one of my projects. I was the project director for a construction project during the COVID-19 pandemic. This pandemic resulted in restricted imports to Australia for months because our international borders were closed. As a result, the delivery of the selected floor tiles was going to be delayed. My conversation with the sponsor went like this:

Me:	"I was advised this morning that the floor tiles will be delayed".
Sponsor:	"Uh-huh." (*awareness and belief*)
Me:	"The supply of the floor tiles is on our critical path".
Sponsor:	"Ok" (*awareness and belief*)
Me:	"That means completion will be delayed by about 6 weeks".
Sponsor:	"What? We can't be delayed that long. We need the building open by October" (*Bingo! Comprehension*)
Sponsor:	"What can we do to avoid the delay?"

This brief exchange not only highlights the difference between knowing, believing and comprehending, but it also leads us to the next important aspect of comprehending.

Just like my sponsor, before any of us can apply our reasoning, decision-making or problem-solving powers to something, we first need to be able to comprehend it [10]. It wasn't until my sponsor comprehended that a '...critical path...' delay meant that the project was going to be late and that he moved into a problem-solving mode ('What can we do to avoid the delay?'). One of the tests that a person is comprehending an issue is a move towards decision-making or problem-solving.

So, how do we move our project teams and stakeholders from knowing and believing to comprehending? Well, primarily through our sense-making, knowledge bridging and storytelling skills. Moving our teams and stakeholders from knowing and believing into comprehending can only be achieved when we create 'shared contextual knowledge' [11]. This happens when we can move the information that *we* know into a frame of reference that *others* can understand.

Creating this shared contextual knowledge is critical to creating a valuable experience for our project teams and stakeholders. Not only does it allow them to comprehend the situation and to apply themselves to decision-making and problems solving, but this shared contextual knowledge allows them to bond more strongly as a group. It is only through shared contextual knowledge that members from different backgrounds, disciplines and networks can begin to understand the actions, goals and intentions of others in the group.

This is why the second C, *comprehension,* is fundamental to value co-creation (Fig. 4.2).

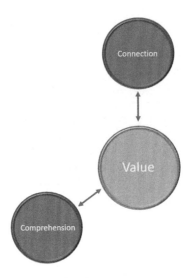

Fig. 4.2 Value co-creation needs comprehension

Collaboration

Collaboration is the third element in our value quartet. You cannot build a truly valuable experience for your project teams and stakeholders without it. Unfortunately, most project managers fail to comprehend that teamwork is *not* collaboration. They are two different things, and if you don't understand the difference, then you probably find that you are building teamwork, without creating collaboration.

Caldicott [12] explains the difference likes this. Suppose you have two teams, Team A and Team B. Both teams consist of two people, a tall man and a short woman. Both teams are given the same objective—to run 100 m as a team within 10 min. The only caveat is that, for the task to be completed successfully, they have to cross the line at the same time as their team-mate.

The man and woman in Team A elected to complete the task by holding each other's hand and running side by side. They easily complete the task within the allotted time. But Team B do things a little differently, they elect to undertake the task as a three-legged race. To complete the task in time, they needed to strap their legs together, put their arms around one another for balance, strategise how they will move together and call out when they are taking each step so that they both don't end up falling over. Team B also completes the task easily. In our example, both Team A and Team B have achieved the same task; however, the experience was markedly different for each of them.

Team A handled the race as a task. Each team member understood their role and completed it successfully. The process was straightforward and relatively uncomplicated. Team A was able to achieve the task without any real need to strategise or communicate. But things were different for Team B. They needed to discuss what they were doing with each other. They were co-joined in the experience so they needed to constantly communicate with one another, provide support to one another and remain in step with each another throughout the entire task.

Team A used teamwork. Both team members did their part to complete the task, but no more. But Team B had to do something more, they had to discover how to run together. They had to learn from each step until they found a natural rhythm. Team B had to shift their thinking from 'What do I have to do to finish?' to 'What do we have to do to finish?'. This shift in thinking '…created a unique coherence in their efforts, a kind of alignment that could actually be repeated the next time they had to run a three-legged race or coach someone else on how to do it…' (p. 7) [12]. In other words, they collaborated.

This simple example highlights the fundamental difference between teamwork and collaboration. Successful teamwork requires you to do your part; successful collaboration requires you to tailor your skills and strengths to align with the skills and strengths of others. The true strength of collaboration, and the key reason why it is intrinsic in the value co-creation experience, is that collaboration releases the power of mutual discovery and learning. True collaboration is a holistic, continuous process, that demands team members engage with one another on a far deeper level than teamwork does.

Now don't get me wrong, there is nothing wrong with teamwork. Teamwork works perfectly well for simple endeavours like playing football or running a 100 m race together. But when faced with complex challenges or wicked problems like projects, collaboration will beat teamwork every day of the week. Collaboration will always create a richer and deeper value experience than teamwork because collaboration is not just about completing the designated task. Collaboration is about the journey of discovery and the learning that takes place when a team overcomes complex challenges together.

To foster value co-creation through our projects, we need to elevate people from the realm of teamwork into the realm of true collaboration. Of course, we can't just go and strap their legs together and make them run a 100 m (as funny as that would be). We need to get them to think differently about what they are doing, and we can do this by employing six strategies:

1. Teach them to see challenges through the eyes of another discipline.
2. Create opportunities for mentoring and coaching within the team.
3. Reframe experiences in multiple contexts, so they are seen from different perspectives.
4. Make it OK to question facts and assumptions so the team can test creative hypothesis together.
5. See challenges as an opportunity for discovery and learning.
6. Reward the collective intelligence of the team, not the brilliance of a single member.

In the end, what we are trying to do is transition our team and stakeholders from a fixed mindset, where they simply apply the knowledge they already have to a specific problem, to a growth mindset, where they are challenged to push themselves to learn something new.

This is why collaboration is intrinsic to value co-creation. The experience of facing challenging and complex situations leads our teams and stakeholders to new discoveries, and the satisfaction of new learning will always surpass that of merely finishing a task (Fig. 4.3).

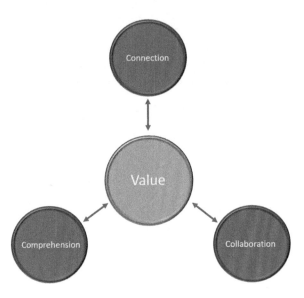

Fig. 4.3 Value co-creation needs collaboration

Coupling

The fourth and final element in our value co-creation model is *coupling*. Coupling is required to make the other 3C's work together to create value. If we have the other 3C's in place, but no coupling, we can end up with a terrible experience for everyone.

Having connection without comprehension or collaboration creates frustration. Having comprehension without connection or collaboration creates apathy. Having collaboration without connection or comprehension creates disaster. Coupling is the glue that binds connection, comprehension and collaboration together. It's the 'missing link' that transforms the first 3C's from potentially destructive powers into a value co-creation experience.

So, what is needed to create this last, important aspect of the value co-creation experience?

Well, in short, you.

To create coupling in your project, you need to have a people-centred view of your project. Understanding the value creation model and being skilled at developing the first three 3C's is not enough. You also need to intuit what is missing from the individual experiences of your project team members and stakeholders and then fill that gap so they can become active participants in the value co-creation process. For some, you will need to help create an emotional connection to the project through your leadership, team building or story-telling skills. For others, you will need to fill in gaps of comprehension through your knowledge bridging, expectation management or sense-making skills. And for others, you need to encourage collaboration through your problem-solving, optioneering or consensus-building skills.

Creating this coupling is not a one-time, one-size-fits-all deal. It requires you to have your finger on the pulse of your project team and stakeholders all the time. Every new challenge changes the game. You need to be deliberately finding new ways to help your team and stakeholders connect, comprehend and collaborate. The only way you can do this is by changing your perspective. You must start seeing your project not as a linked group of tasks that need to be accomplished on time, under budget and to a required level of quality but as a system for value co-creation (Fig. 4.4).

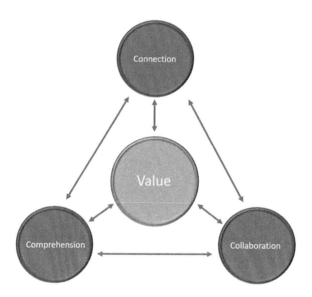

Fig. 4.4 Value co-creation needs coupling

References

1. Winter M, Smith C, Morris P, Cicmil S (2006) Directions for future research in project management: the main findings of a UK government-funded research network. Int J Proj Manag 24(8):638–649
2. Laursen M, Svejvig P (2016) Taking stock of project value creation: a structured literature review with future directions for research and practice. Int J Proj Manag 34(4):736–747
3. Lyotard J-F (1983) The differend: phrases in dispute (trans: Georges Van Den Abbeele). University of Minnesota Press, Minneapolis
4. Usher G, Whitty SJ (2017) Project Management Yinyang: coupling project success and client satisfaction. Proj Manage Res Pract 4

5. Cohen DJ, Graham RJ (2001) The project manager's MBA: how to translate project decisions into business success. Wiley
6. Normann R, Ramirez R (1993) From value chain to value constellation: designing interactive strategy. Harv Bus Rev 71(4):65–77
7. Stegnor J. (n.d.) Gloves on the boardroom table. https://primarygoals.com/teams/books/heart-of-change/gloves-on-boardroom-table/
8. Usher GS (2019) Creating confidence amongst complexity: the 'lived experience' of client-side project managers in the Australian construction sector. Ph.D., Business and Management, University of Southern Queensland, Brisbane, Australia
9. Usher GS, Whitty SJ (2018) The client-side project manager: a practitioner of design. Proj Manage Res Pract 5:6147
10. Bourget D (2017) The role of consciousness in grasping and understanding. Philos Phenomenol Res 95(2):285–318
11. Weick KE (2016) 60th anniversary essay. Adm Sci Q 61(3)
12. Caldicott SM (2012) Midnight lunch: the 4 phases of team collaboration success from Thomas Edison's Lab. Wiley

Closing Thoughts

5

Time to Come Clean

Throughout this book, I have done my best to undermine your current understanding of project management theory and practice. I've shown you the holes in traditional project management theory and how they got there. I've explained why the current definition of project management is woefully inadequate. And I've done my best to show you that project management is about so much more than just 'managing projects'—it's also about the project eco-system and a value co-creation experience, both of which seem to be completely ignored in most project management literature and education.

From all this, you might conclude that I think we should throw out everything we currently know about project management and just start again. But nothing could be further from the truth. So, I guess it's time for me to come clean because, despite everything I've said in this book, I am actually a big fan of the way we currently manage projects.

Why? Because it works.

If I have learned anything in my 20 years of managing projects, it's that, for all our flaws and foibles, we are a pragmatic bunch. We don't have time to waste on things that don't work. The reason we keep creating Gantt charts or measuring success against time, cost and scope is because these things continue to assist us to deliver our projects. They help us '...act when we cannot foresee consequences...plan when we cannot know...and organise what we cannot control...' [1].

So, despite all the challenges I see with our current understanding of project management, I find myself reaching the same conclusions that the Rethinking Project Management Network [2] did:

> ...that the extant project management body of thought is [not] worthless and should [not] be abandoned, but rather [it should be] enrich[ed] and extend[ed]... (p. 639)

The problems we face in our profession right now are not because everything is wrong. They exist because we haven't seen the whole elephant yet. So, our challenge as modern project managers is to be open to the idea that our current perception is flawed and be willing to admit that our perspective needs to change.

We need to be courageous enough to explore new ideas about what we do. We need to acknowledge that, although we might be experts in the current methodologies, frameworks and processes of project management, this is only half the story. We need to step up and start questioning the way we, and ultimately our teams, stakeholders and sponsor see our profession. We must be bold enough to challenge the expectation that the hard paradigm of time, cost and scope is all that matters. In short, we must be willing to submit our profession to a revolution of thought and practice.

Oh, You're a Project Manager; That's Nice. What Do You Do?

So how does everything we now know help with my initial problem? How does it help my inability to succinctly explain the complexities of our job to someone who doesn't really understand project management? Well, now these conversations go something like this:

Partygoer: *"So, Greg, what do you do?"*
Me: *"I'm a project manager".*
Partygoer   *"Oh, a lot of people seem to be project managers these days. What exactly does a project manager do?"*
Me: *"We create value by leading a group of people who have never worked together before on a journey that no one has ever taken before to achieve something that no one has ever done before".*
Partygoer: *"Oh, so like a tour guide?"*
Me: *[mental eye-roll] "Yes, like a tour guide".*

But then, from somewhere across the room, someone else hears the exchange. The only other project manager at the party looks up from her wine. She catches my eye, tips her wine glass in my direction and gives the slightest of head nods. She gets it, even if I can't really explain it to the others. And who knows, maybe the others will never really comprehend what that explanation truly means, but that's OK. At least I now feel my explanation captures the complexity and enormity of our role. And for now, that will have to do.

References

1. La Porte TR (1975) Complexity and uncertainty: challenge to action. In: Organized social complexity: challenge to politics and policy. Princeton University Press, Princeton, NJ, pp 332–356
2. Winter M, Smith C, Morris P, Cicmil S (2006) Directions for future research in project management: the main findings of a UK government-funded research network. Int J Proj Manag 24(8):638–649

Printed in Great Britain
by Amazon

56132092R00071